LISA R

THE
UPSIDE
OF
DOWN
TIMES

DISCOVERING
THE POWER OF
GRATITUDE

DENVER, COLORADO

Outskirts Press, Inc.
http://www.outskirtspress.com

ISBN: 978-1-4327-9055-4

Outskirts Press and the "OP" logo are trademarks belonging to Outskirts Press, Inc.

PRINTED IN THE UNITED STATES OF AMERICA

For my amazing husband, Scott.

Thank you for loving me, supporting me and cheering me on.

I could not have done any of this without you.

I love you with all my heart and appreciate you more every day.

Contents

Chapter 4: Wealth

Bonus Section

A New Beginning: Choosing Gratitude

Hire Lisa Ryan for your next event

Acknowledgements:

Thank you mom and dad for your never ending encouragement and belief in my abilities. Thank you Patty for being my sounding board, cheerleader and BFF. Thank you Catherine Foster for your friendship and our partnership in the Positive Thinkers Network. Thank you Dick Clough for helping me invent the name for my company and getting everything off the ground. Thank you Robin Jay for coming into my life and casting me in "The Keeper of the Keys." Thank you Laura Vobornik for introducing me to Robin. Thank you Chris King for getting me started on the positive thinking path. Thank you Mike Gleba, Angie Hall and Dan Hall for getting me started with my gratitude practice.

Thank you to everyone who shared their gratitude stories with me: Colleen Bruemmer, Cassidy Chapman, Darren Cross, Michelle Cunningham, Linda Davidson, Emily Drake, Rich Fercy, Greg Kozera, Ali Palecek, Jori Reijonen, Ph.D, Scott Roman, Larry Rudolph, Laura Rusick, Mary Beth Sammon, Sam Scheer, Ann Shipley, Bill Truax, and Christine Zust

Thank you to my amazing editor AJ Copywriting & Editing. Your talent, skill and insight helped bring everything together.

"There are few finer excesses in the world than an excess of gratitude."
— **Jean de la Bruyere**

The downside of life is that too much gratitude is not something we usually have to contend with. Most people tend to focus on the negative and many don't receive nearly as much acknowledgement as they would like. Chances are also pretty good that we don't give as much recognition as we should.

Now for the upside.

Harnessing the power of gratitude can make a positive change in our lives and well as in the lives of others, and can ultimately lead us to healthier, more successful, and wealthier lives.

Struggling to overcome some ill-timed events in my own life (like a career loss and my father's severe stroke), I learned that practicing gratefulness could help me through experiences which otherwise might have been unbearable.

This book is a product of how the power of gratitude has had a profound impact on my life. Through gratefulness, I attracted the love of my life and created the business of my dreams.

When people hear the words "power of gratitude," they often view it as a rather "fluffy" subject. Easy, silly and even unnecessary. Dr. Robert Emmons, of the University of California, Davis, one of the world's foremost researchers on gratitude, says, "Far from being a warm, fuzzy sentiment, gratitude is morally and intellectually demanding. It requires contemplation, reflection, and discipline and can be hard work." While there is certainly a spiritual bent to gratitude, the science is indisputable.

To keep from getting 'fluffy', we'll look at things from both a scientific and a personal standpoint. There will be plenty of anecdotes which show how giving thanks has worked in a variety of situations – while providing solid scientific evidence to reinforce every story.

Ready to begin?

Introduction

Welcome to a journey of self-exploration - and no, you don't have to keep your arms and legs inside the ride at all times; let's have some fun!

This book will S.H.O.W. you how gratefulness can positively impact four major areas of your life.

- "S" is for Self - gratitude improves your attitude and outlook

- "H" is for Health - improved physical health results from appreciation.

- "O" is for Others - acknowledgement influences and improves our relationships

- "W" is for Wealth - gratefulness has a positive impact on your bottom line.

Getting the most out of this book does not require naturally positive thinking or being a Pollyanna. Simply keep an open mind, try some of the suggestions for yourself, and you'll notice the changes that are bound to happen in your life.

Though, I should probably forewarn you, gratitude is not for wimps.

Note: you'll see a few symbols throughout this book.

 Here's a tip

 Gratitude journal information/instructions

 Denotes research and studies

 Shows you when it's your turn to take action

INTRODUCTION

"We are more starved for appreciation,
than we are for bread."
– Mother Teresa

In 2011, I co-founded a networking group called "The Positive Thinkers Network." We conducted our first meeting expecting about 20-30 people to come. Instead, eighty-nine showed up. Because we didn't realize the value of having attendees pay in advance, the wait staff had to handle eighty-nine separate checks. One of the waiters, Darren, was extraordinary. He never missed a beat and always had a smile on his face.

I noticed Darren at other networking events with similar results; an outgoing personality, a big smile, and always willing to go the extra mile to serve…leaving all in attendance with a positive experience.

A few weeks later, my husband and I dined at the restaurant where Darren worked and we were lucky enough to have him as our waiter. His service was magnificent as usual.

On the way out of the restaurant, I asked the maître de for the general manager's card. He imparted a concerned look that said, "What do you want it for?" Nevertheless, I took the card and we went home.

I wrote the general manager a thank-you card and told him he should be proud to have someone of Darren's caliber on his staff. I stuck it in the mail and forgot about it.

At our next Positive Thinker's Network luncheon at his establishment, Darren greeted me with a big smile and hug. Then, he handed me this:

THE UPSIDE OF DOWN TIMES

A Poem To Lisa Ryan

Positive thinking
Is a life raft to the soul
When you feel like your ship is sinking…

A positive outlook each day
Invites God's special blessings
To come your way…

Lisa, I can say with all positivity
Your act of kindness to my heart
Has forever inspired me…

My way of thanking you
Will be to pass on that beautiful positive vibe
In all you say and do…

It's amazing how one person's sunshine
Can incredibly change another's life
And it makes me proud to say, you're a friend of mine.

God bless you,
Darren

Darren's note is a treasure, and he is truly a blessing in my life. Every one of us possesses the power to make such a difference with the people we connect with on a daily basis. In turn, it affects our lives as well.

☞ Who has provided extraordinary service to you lately? Take a few minutes and write a note to the individual's manager or to

INTRODUCTION

the server themselves. Express your gratitude for the service you received. There is not a better way to make a person's day.

I wrote the note to _____ on (date): _____

Taking the time to write it made me feel:

_____

_____

_____

_____

_____

_____

_____

_____

_____

_____

_____

_____

_____

_____

_____

_____

_____

_____

_____

_____

_____

_____

_____

_____

THE UPSIDE OF DOWN TIMES

"When a person doesn't have gratitude,
something is missing in his or her humanity.
A person can almost be defined by his or
her attitude toward gratitude."
— **Elie Wiesel**

If our humanity can be defined by our attitude towards thankfulness, how then do we characterize gratitude? Webster defines it as "the state of being grateful," while Wikipedia defines it as a "positive emotion or attitude in acknowledgment of a benefit that one has received or will receive."

The word gratitude comes from the Latin root "gratia," meaning "favor, grace, and esteem" and "gratus" meaning "pleasing, welcome, and beloved." All of its derivatives involve kindness, generosity, gifts, and the beauty of giving and receiving. In other words, gratitude is a darn good thing!

The YOU! series authors, Dr. Mehmet Oz and Dr. Mike Roizen described five attributes of genuine thankfulness: They believe that gratitude gives you an opportunity to **exercise emotions**; it's found **in the details**; it's **not the same as I-owe-you-one**; it's **not a now-and-then thing**; and it's **not for wimps**.

Let's consider how appreciation gives us the opportunity to **exercise our emotions**. True gratitude is not just arbitrarily uttering a hasty "thank you" as the waitress fills your glass of iced tea. Gratitude is when it's 85°F outside with 90% humidity, and you have built up a powerful thirst. The waitress fills up your glass with iced tea, and as you take that first delightful gulp, you can shout from your heart, "THANK YOU!" FEEL the emotion from your head to your toes. You experience what it's like to be truly grateful to quench your thirst.

"One of the reasons why gratitude works so well is that it connects us with others," theorizes Dr. Michael McCollough, of the Southern Methodist University in Dallas, Texas. "That's why when you give thanks, it should be more heartfelt and personal instead of a terse thank-you note for a gift or a hastily run-through grace before dinner."

Because the mind cannot experience two opposite emotions at the same time, it's important to keep yourself in a state of gratitude as often as you can. For instance, the next time you are having a bad day, take a moment to think about something that you're grateful for and you will start to move into a happier place. As the Buddha once said, "Let us rise up and be thankful, for if we didn't learn a lot today, at least we learned a little; and if we didn't learn a little, at least we didn't get sick; and if we got sick, at least we didn't die. So, let us all be thankful." A little bit of grace goes a long way to help us exercise our emotions.

Gratitude is **in the details**. When you let people know that you appreciate them, offer specific reasons why. Expand your comments from "Thanks" to "Thanks so much for helping me put together this report. You really helped to make the project successful. I appreciate you." The power of the thank you is in the details. It will not only make you feel good, the person you are thanking will know specifically what he or she did well—and chances are, he or she will do an even better job next time.

When thanking others, tell them that you appreciate them AND whatever they did to help you. Acknowledge the person as well as the task and you will build a stronger relationship.

Sharing gratitude is **not the same as "I owe you one."** When you feel indebted to someone, it's different from the emotional bond you create with pure, open gratitude. Drs. Roizen and Oz reveal, "It takes emotional honesty and a little bit of vulnerability to make that spot inside you melt." We are grateful to others because we feel it, and we want to express our heartfelt sentiments. When someone does something nice for you, accept it in the manner it was given—with pure intent. When you feel obligated to someone, you do not experience the same connection and closeness with that person. When someone does something nice for you, give him or her a genuine "thank you." When someone thanks you, reply with "You're welcome." That's it; just enjoy the feeling without obligation. Of course, this doesn't mean that you should keep taking without ever giving back—that's not the way we succeed in our relationships.

Speaking of saying, "You're welcome," make sure you actually utter those words. When a person says, "Thank you," he or she is giving you a gift. When you say, "It's no problem," "It's nothing," "Don't worry about it," etc., it's the same as taking that gift and throwing it back. Accept the gift with a simple, "You're welcome." That's enough.

In addition, gratitude is **not a now-and-then thing**. We need a consistent practice of acknowledgement to keep our appreciation muscles strong. Activities such as these: keeping a gratitude journal, sending thank-you notes and cards to loved ones, consistently acknowledging and appreciating our lives— when we practice regularly, we have the ability to access gratitude when we need it.

We have no idea how much a single smile, a kind word, or an approving comment means to someone. It only takes a couple seconds, yet the impact on our relationships with others

INTRODUCTION

is profound. Make a point to bring a smile to at least one person today.

Today, I brought a smile to_____.

From this experience, I learned:

_____

_____

_____

_____

_____

_____

_____

_____

_____

_____

_____

_____

_____

_____

_____

_____

_____

_____

_____

_____

THE UPSIDE OF DOWN TIMES

"Change is inevitable. Growth is optional."
— Unknown

The last attribute written about by Drs. Roizen and Oz is **gratitude is not for wimps.** It's very easy to be grateful when things are going well. It's not so easy when in the midst of challenges. In other words, when we are going through a difficult time, it can be more difficult to look at the situation from an appreciative perspective. That's why gratitude is a PRACTICE. Just as counting one's blessings is not a "now-and-then thing," our consistent practice will strengthen our gratitude muscle and help us when we need it the most.

Maybe the thought of being grateful for all things in your life never really crossed your mind. Now that you are aware of the power of gratitude, you're moving into the **"conscious incompetence"** stage. It is at this point that you know what you don't know. An example would be learning to tie shoes. A child may know that he needs to learn to tie his shoes, but he doesn't know how to do it. Mom or dad still needs to help.

When you start your gratitude practice, you may feel uncomfortable. It's a new way of thinking and it hasn't become a habit yet. Congratulations, you are now "consciously competent." In this stage of development, the child can tie his shoes, but it takes a lot of thought to do so.

Before long, you'll learn to harness the power of gratitude in every area of your life - and you'll do it subconsciously. You have reached the pinnacle - "unconscious competence." This is when the child doesn't even think about shoe tying, he just does it. Practice

INTRODUCTION

gratitude long enough and it will become as natural to you as tying your shoes.

In my journey towards unconscious competence, I found that gratitude was not for wimps the hard way. About a year after starting my gratitude journal, I experienced my first major challenge.

In a tough economy, job loss is a common occurrence. Many of my friends and associates found themselves on the wrong end of a corporate restructuring and were currently on the job market. It never occurred to me that I would soon be joining them.

I was working in medical sales, having a record year after several of my large deals closed, and was well on the way to winning the annual award trip. My job offered everything a rep could possible want - great money, company car, fabulous benefits, and all my expenses paid. Even gasoline was included in the package. Life was good.

It was Monday morning when an invitation was sent out to the staff to attend an "Organizational Announcement" conference call at 11:00 the next day. Now, what would you do if you received that same message? Would you calmly sit by and wait to learn the news on the phone call, or would you call all your friends to see if anyone knew what was going on – Who was getting canned? Who was getting promoted? I chose the latter and discovered that no one knew a thing; it really was the company's best kept secret.

On the morning of the fateful call, one of my friends informed me that the call had been switched to 11:30. I said, "Oh, I didn't get that e-mail." To which she replied, "You weren't on the list." Ouch.

THE UPSIDE OF DOWN TIMES

With bated breath, I called in at 11:00 to hear the big news. At approximately 11:08, the call commenced with the VP of Sales and VP of Human Resources finally getting on the line. The call went something like this: "The company is going through severe financial problems right now. We're going to lose $10 million this year. Your position has been eliminated, effective immediately. Please stay off the phone so our outplacement firm can get a hold of you. We're not going to answer any questions; you'll have to wait until you get your FedEx package tomorrow and then HR will contact you. Goodbye."

To say I was blindsided would be an understatement. I devoted seven years of heart and soul to that company and yet no one was acknowledged by name. There were no words of appreciation for the years of service, or even an admission that this was a difficult decision for the organization. As a matter of fact, there was nothing on the call that slightly indicated that it was not just a recorded message. Trembling uncontrollably from head to toe, my shock turned to irrepressible sobbing. This was a definite 'down time' in my career.

After my heart-rending pity party, which lasted several hours, the thought came to me, "Lisa, you've been giving talks on the power of gratitude for over a year now; you know what you need to do." I asked myself, "What is it about this situation that you can be grateful for? Where's the upside?"

I sat in the silence listening to what my inner voice was trying to tell me. In my mind's eye, a piece of paper appeared: my goal list from 1989. The very first items on this list included becoming a professional inspirational speaker as well as a published author. At that moment the realization hit me - the Universe must feel that I was much more ready to move on to achieving my dreams than I had believed. The opportunity of a lifetime was being presented, and I was eager to move forward.

As time passed, it struck me that the phone call was the best thing that could have happened to me, not the worst. There were a lot of issues in the company that didn't sit well with me, and due to some changes in management and corporate philosophy, my job was not as enjoyable as it used to be. My side businesses – speaking, writing, and a few home-based ventures – offered a lot more fun, but until the decision was made for me, I probably never would have left medical sales. My income and my way of life were far too comfortable.

For years, my dream was to go out on my own and pursue a speaking career. I would get cocky at times thinking, "Oh yeah, I'm going to build up my speaking business and quit my job..." Yeah, right. Leaving my job sounded good in theory, but because of the money and the awesome benefits, resigning was not a viable option. When the unexpected termination occurred, it was time for me to trust my gut and go for it. After all these years, I could finally pursue my lifelong goals.

Admittedly, it wasn't all wine and roses along the way. There was anger: "How could they do that to ME?" There were days of feeling depressed and totally abandoned by my co-workers. There were exhilarating days, joyful days, and days of being flat-out scared: "What am I going to DO with my life really?" But, every time I got out of my head and back to my heart, I realized that the required resources came to me exactly at the time they were needed.

I soon discovered that the "upside" of being unemployed in a "down" economy was that the door had been unceremoniously flung open, and it was up to me to create what was on the other side.

THE UPSIDE OF DOWN TIMES

Several lifelong goals have already been accomplished. I am the founder of Grategy® and the Co-founder of the Positive Thinkers Network. As a nationally recognized speaker and a published author of the book "With Excellence," I have appeared in two documentaries sharing my expertise on the topic of gratitude. The movies, "The Keeper of the Keys" and "The Gratitude Experiment" feature other world-renowned experts as well. It's been a fun ride and it just keeps getting better! Gratefulness has supported me through the down times of unemployment and has helped me envision the opportunities which lie ahead.

My job loss was difficult, but I got through it. It's one thing to lose your source of income, and it's quite another when someone you love faces a health crisis. In this case, practicing appreciation can be almost impossible.

Almost a year had gone by, when my gratitude muscle was challenged again. It was a sunny Saturday morning and my husband and I were getting ready to take a trip downtown to see the set where a major movie was being filmed. We were on our way out the door when the phone rang. A man who I did not know informed me that he was with my father. My dad was in a state of confusion and couldn't talk. I told the man on the phone to hang up immediately and call 9-1-1, as I believed my father was having a stroke. Instead of enjoying our trip downtown, we raced to the hospital where we spent the rest of that day.

A few hours after my dad was admitted, the "stranger," Larry, came by to check on him. I questioned him as to how he knew my dad, and found out that Larry was a Jehovah's Witness who had been visiting my dad every week for the past two years. Larry is an extraordinarily caring man whose mission was visiting and checking in on the elderly.

INTRODUCTION

It was Larry who first suspected there was something wrong with my dad, because when he called him that morning to make sure he'd be home for his weekly visit, my father couldn't speak. Larry went to the house and urged my dad to unlock the front door so he could see what was going on. It took my dad about ten minutes to open the door. Larry rushed inside and sat my dad down. He then proceeded to get my dad's phone book to call family for help.

I am incredibly grateful to Larry – not only for caring enough about my dad to check in regularly, but to tend to him when he needed it. If it had not been for Larry, my dad might not be with us today. If it weren't for the power of gratitude, I might not be able to get past the shock and sadness of my father's stroke to thank Larry for being there for him and calling us when he did.

According to his doctor, dad's stroke was a "significant" one, affecting the left side of his brain, where the ability to speak and reason resides. He also had some paralysis on his right side. My father had had a stroke three years earlier, but had completely recovered from it. This stroke extended from the original one, making it much worse the second time around.

This was an extraordinarily difficult time for my entire family. Days consisted of trips to the hospital, working with social workers and therapists, paying his bills, keeping up with his house and yard work, and managing all of his financial affairs.

My father struggled in his therapy. He worked hard, yet became frustrated with his slow progress. It was heartbreaking for all of us.

When asking myself the question, "What can I be grateful for in this situation?" the answer came slowly. At least my father is still alive.

THE UPSIDE OF DOWN TIMES

Stroke is the third leading cause of death in the US, with almost 150,000 people dying each year from strokes. Many of my friends lost their parents due to this or other ailments, and I still have my dad. I feel blessed. Because the stroke affected the left side of his brain, my father had a great deal of difficulty speaking. When it first happened, he couldn't speak at all. As his language skills progressed, he would begin to say something and then lose his train of thought. He was incapable of finding the words he wanted to say. He would start a sentence with the words, "There's something personal I need to tell you...," I would lean forward, anticipating some kind of revelation, and then his mind went blank and he could not continue. In those instances, his default phrases became "Thank you", and "I just want you to let you know how much I love you."

The fact that even in such difficult circumstances, my father was able to get to gratitude shows what kind of man he is. He is strong, has a positive attitude, a beautiful smile, and he is a blessing to all he comes into contact with. As for me, the precious moments we spend together will forever be savored.

Remember that job loss I fretted over? Well, now I realize that I am even more grateful for it, because I am able to devote more time to my dad. We haven't spent this much time together since my childhood.

When someone you love is experiencing a health challenge, it's important to be there to support him or her. It's also critical that you take care of yourself along the way. Finding little things for which you can be grateful in the situation helps to get you through even the most difficult times.

INTRODUCTION

My relationship with my siblings has strengthened as we have all bonded to get through this ordeal together. Immediately after our father's stroke, my out-of-state brother and sister came in to spend time with him. My other two sisters and I visited regularly to keep him company, attend his therapy sessions with him and cheer him on. I'm so grateful that we were all present to love and support our father, and it has helped us in return.

When we practice counting blessings in a systematic way, we change our brains, especially those areas already wired for negativity. Dr. Robert Emmons explains, "When you express a feeling, you amplify it. When you express anger, you get angrier; when you express gratitude, you become more grateful."

Though in the beginning, I might have felt it to be nearly impossible to be appreciative, in the end I believe there are many things to be grateful for. My father receives amazing treatment from his professional caregivers. With speech therapy, physical therapy, and occupational therapy, my dad's recovery is proceeding nicely. He now resides in a retirement facility where he receives wonderful care. He appreciates everything the staff does to assist him and he acknowledges them with his smile and words of thanks. In return, everyone at the retirement facility loves him. On Valentine's Day, the residents voted him "Valentine's Day King." I was told he won by a landslide.

It's a blessing that my dad is still with us and we as a family do not take that fact for granted. Linda shared that her life changed profoundly when her mother died unexpectedly at a young age. Through her experience, she learned that it's critical to appreciate people while they are alive, instead of eulogizing them when they're gone. Linda and her family make it a point to say, "I love you" whenever they hang up the phone. It doesn't matter how short the conversation, they want to make sure that in case this is the last conversation ever had with that person, it's a good one. By incorporating love and kindness into her family interactions, she has found more joy in her life.

Whether you are going through down times as the result of the ill health, or passing of a loved one, loss of a job, or any other "negative" situation, in the direst of circumstances, it's important to find ways to give thanks. Gratitude is one of the easiest emotions to access because when we look hard enough, we can always find an upside. Even if it's just a small thing, it's a start. Once you begin to consciously look for positive people, events, and circumstances to acknowledge, life improves. Realizing that gratitude is not for wimps makes it critical to exercise your appreciation muscle regularly so that it's strong when you need it.

☞ Before we move on, take a minute now and think of your own "not for wimps" story. Have you or someone in your family lost their source of income which is leading to financial difficulties? Has an important relationship ended? Are you experiencing health issues? Whatever it is, ask yourself the question, "What can I be grateful for in this situation?" If you can't think of an answer, imagine what it would be like if you could be grateful. Write down your answers and add to the list as needed. This exercise may not be a cure-all, but it will help you to feel a bit better.

_____

_____

_____

_____

_____

INTRODUCTION

_____

_____

_____

_____

_____

_____

_____

_____

_____

_____

_____

_____

_____

_____

_____

_____

_____

_____

_____

_____

_____

_____

Now that you understand some of the attributes of gratitude, let me S.H.O.W. you four areas where it can make a huge difference in the quality of your life—your SELF, your HEALTH, your relationships with OTHERS, and your WEALTH.

Chapter 1

Self

The Power of a Thankful Attitude

*"Cultivate an attitude of gratitude, of giving and forgiving.
Nothing can bring you peace but yourself."*
– **Ralph Waldo Emerson**

Let's begin with the self; after all, it's all about us anyway, isn't it? You've undoubtedly heard the airline safety instructions to put on your own oxygen mask first. In an airplane as well as in life, this is a necessary action. We need to take care of ourselves first. If we don't pay attention to ourselves, we won't have the opportunity to look after others. The same is true when it comes to gratitude. No one can force us to be grateful; we have to choose to appreciate what we have in our lives.

The power of giving thanks is transformational.

I didn't start out with the goal of making a living as a gratitude expert. My journey began by simply creating a thankfulness log as a result of a seminar attended with friends. Of all the books, seminars, workshops, and intensive study completed over the years, my gratitude journal has been the single most life-changing action I have ever taken.

I have always been a self-professed "self-development junkie."

SELF

Reading Napoleon Hill's, *Think and Grow Rich* and attending my first Dale Carnegie class in the late 1980s, got me off to a running start. Unfortunately, in the course of attending the workshops and reading the books, a pattern emerged. (For those of you similarly inclined, see if this sounds familiar?) On day one, I would be hyped up – excited, passionate, and anxiously putting into practice all of the principals learned. After a short period of time, it would become apparent that my coworkers, friends, and family were not necessarily impressed with my newfound enthusiasm. Soon, my spirit would start to dampen, but I would press on for a while longer. In the end, I would find myself back at square one, grousing along with everyone else. How frustrating! I grew tired of the constant backtracking and searched for a way to keep the magic alive.

After attending a four-day intensive workshop with three friends, we were all ready to keep the energy within us thriving. The seminar was everything that we could have hoped for – and more. Not only did the seminar involve a fire walk – yes, an actual walk across fire – we learned significant skills to help us achieve our goals, take better care of our health, and enjoy a fresh outlook. (This was actually my second fire walk – I like to tell people that I feel the need to walk across hot coals every twenty years, whether I needed to or not. But actually, I just wanted to do it again with my friends.)

The four of us were motivated to make this seminar different from all the others – a true transformational experience. We didn't want to retreat into our old habits, so we figured out a way we could continue to connect on a daily basis and keep the teachings alive.

We opened an e-mail thread on Facebook, and every day we shared three reflections from the seminar – people we met, experiences we had, lessons we learned. We also wrote down 3-5 things that we were grateful for. We did this every day and we held each other accountable. As we moved further and further away from the seminar, the daily reflections ceased, but the gratitude continued because it was fun to share. The e-mail thread eventually ended as everyone's life got in the way. However, I kept up my own practice because I enjoyed taking a few minutes every day giving thanks.

In the beginning of my personal gratitude practice, I purchased a "real" journal. It had a fancy cover, beautiful quotes, and a ribbon marker. There was plenty of room for daily introspection; sometimes the spaces were enough, sometimes they weren't. Because the book was so lovely, it made me want to strive for perfection in my daily writings. The pressure to achieve excellence soon became overwhelming and my journaling fell to the wayside.

Soon after stopping, my mood became noticeably more negative. I was getting frustrated easily and started taking the good things in my life for granted. Spending a few precious moments being grateful had been making a difference after all. I quickly realized it wasn't the kind of journal I used, but as long as I was writing down daily a few things I appreciated, it could help me.

My current gratitude journal is a binder with loose-leaf pages in it. When I resumed the habit, my writing became less fancy and more real. In journaling, perfection is not the point – you have to be you! Upon awakening, I jot down 3-5 things for which I am appreciative. Pertinent details are added to my statements. For example, instead of simply writing "I am grateful for Scott," I write: "I am grateful that Scott cooked a great dinner last night." Writing down "I am grateful for Scott, I am grateful for my house, I am grateful for my cats," etc. every day would get old very quickly. Adding details deepens the sensation of gratitude.

Noticing people or situations for which I am grateful throughout the day has become a habit. Relishing the sunshine, the flowers, a cat curled up on my lap, or the warmth and comfort of my bed makes me appreciate the small joys of life. Often, saying "thanks" out loud during the day when something good happens reminds me to journal it the next morning.

☞ What areas in your life would improve if you incorporated a gratitude practice? Consider taking one step today to make appreciation a ritual in at least one part of your day.

_____

_____

_____

_____

_____

_____

_____

_____

_____

_____

_____

_____

_____

_____

_____

_____

_____

_____

THE UPSIDE OF DOWN TIMES

"In the river of life...the soul enters the body at the river's edge and there begins a superb journey. Some are content to merely wade in the shallows near the shore. Others venture into deeper water to see how it feels to be buoyant and to swim."
– Unknown

Solid evidence supports the science of gratitude - actually much more than I could have imagined.

The first book I read was *Thanks* by Dr. Robert Emmons. Dr. Emmons is a PhD researcher out of the University of California, Davis. He has conducted many research projects in the field, which became the basis for additional study. In one of his most popular experiments, a random group of students was divided into three. The first group wrote down the things for which they were thankful every day (gratitude group). The second group wrote down all of the hassles, all of the little things that bothered them on a daily basis (hassles group). The third group simply recorded the day's happenings without positive or negative emotion (control group). After ten weeks, the gratitude group felt 25% happier. You may be asking, "Lisa, how could Dr. Emmons honestly tell that the gratitude group was 25% happier?"

Before the study began, the group of students kept a detailed journal that recorded their feelings on a daily basis – energy level, headaches, pains, attitude, etc. Dr. Emmons wanted to be able to distinguish the chronically happy people from the chronically miserable people. (You know exactly who these people are, right?) Based on this prior research, Dr. Emmons was able to determine that the gratitude group was indeed 25% happier than the other two.

He also found that the gratitude group exercised on average 1.5 hours more per week than the other two groups. They complained less often. They had fewer physical ailments. They were more joyful, enthusiastic, determined, and aware. Interestingly, he then interviewed the family and friends of the gratitude group and asked them if they had noticed any difference. They did, finding the gratitude group to be more emotionally available, as well as nicer to be around.

But wait, there's more! The gratitude group also reported spending less time awake before falling asleep, sleeping more soundly, and feeling greatly refreshed in the morning. What's the moral to this lesson? Count your blessings, not sheep.

Keep some kind of gratitude journal – an appreciation list with details and/or stories. If there's nothing else you take away from this book, know that an appreciation journal is the single most important habit you can have to harness the power of thankfulness in your life.

Kick your log entries up a notch by adding details to your descriptions. If you're just listing words – spouse, house, car, cat, clothes, etc.–it gets boring fast. You can also change the language of gratitude, using starter phrases such as "I am so happy and grateful for…,""I appreciate…," "I am thrilled with…," and "I love…" It's your journal; personalize it to resonate with you and treat it with care.

After you've decided to begin your journal, your next step is to pick the time of day you'll be writing in it. Choosing a regular time is best, as it gets you into the habit – and you'll notice when you don't do it.

One of the main advantages of morning writing is that you get it done. It sets the precedent for a positive start to the day. Upon awakening, think of 3-5 things for which you are grateful. You can reflect on the previous day and the good things that happened. You can give thanks for the things you have right now: waking up in a warm bed or having a good night's sleep. You can also be grateful for events happening IN ADVANCE. Since the mind cannot tell a lie from a truth, you have the power to "make up" how you want your day to go. Visualize and write down all the good that you imagine will be coming to you during the day and you'll be amazed at how much of it does occur.

Make sure everything is in the present tense and it's what you WANT, not what you DON'T WANT. For example, "I am thankful for a great meeting with my client today" is better than "I am grateful I didn't lose my top client today." See the difference? In the first instance, the mind hears "great meeting" and in the second it hears, "lose top client." You always want to concentrate on stating things in the positive so your subconscious knows what you really want.

As an additional inspiration to start your morning, here is one of my favorite poems from an unknown author:

This is the beginning of a new day.
God has given me this day to use as I will.
I can waste it or use it for good,
but what I do today is important
because I am exchanging a day of my life for it.
When tomorrow comes, this day will be gone forever,
leaving in its place something that I have traded for it.
I want it to be gain and not loss;
good and not evil;
success and not failure;
in order that I shall not regret the price I have paid for it.

SELF

In her book *Happy for No Reason*, Marci Shimoff tells the story of Theresa, a friend of hers who was going through a rough time: a painful divorce, her mother's death, and moving in with her father. They were about "as glum as two people could be." They had both heard from friends that gratitude was supposed to make them feel better, so they thought they'd try it. Each morning, they would share three things in their lives for which they were grateful. The first morning was tough, and they both had a hard time coming up with even one thing. Finally, Theresa looked around the room and saw a vase that she liked. She said that she was thankful for how pretty the vase was; it was the best she could do.

As time went on, they realized they had a lot of things for which they could be grateful – they just had to open their eyes and look around. Their ritual got easier, and their mornings became a lot happier. They eventually found so many things to share that they had to stop before they were done so Theresa wouldn't be late for work. They even added singing *Oh, What a Beautiful Morning* to their repertoire and enjoyed the beginnings of their day immensely.

This story is important because it beautifully demonstrates the power of doing what you can, where you are, with what you have—even if it's just appreciating a pretty vase.

We've all had mornings when we wake up on the wrong side of the bed and can't think of a single thing for which we are grateful. It's on those days that we need to remind ourselves to start small. Be thankful your bed is comfortable and the sun is shining. Be thankful that you're breathing on your own (after all, there are a lot of people who aren't). Once you get started – especially if it's something silly, you laugh – you get on a roll and it gets easier.

THE UPSIDE OF DOWN TIMES

☞ Sharing your gratitude with a loved one is a powerful way to start the day. Writing your acknowledgements gives them power. When you begin to write, get yourself into a state of total appreciation. Smile. The more involved your senses, the better. Take the time and fully express your feelings of appreciation. Spend two to five minutes in gratitude today and experience a profound impact on your energy.

Right now I am grateful for: _____

_____

_____

_____

_____

_____

_____

_____

_____

_____

_____

_____

_____

_____

_____

_____

_____

_____

_____

_____

SELF

"Do your practice patiently and consistently with no thought of the result, and the process will deliver outstanding rewards in due time."
– D. Trinidad Hunt

Cassidy attended one of my Grategy® workshops and shared her discovery in the power of the journaling process: "Your message was particularly meaningful to me. I am normally a very spirited and upbeat person; however, life has been very difficult lately. It's easy to lose sight that even when everything is hard, and you really just want to cry, there are still things to be thankful for. I went right back to my office and started a journal. I have already noticed that it made a difference in my day. Yesterday was a very stressful day, and one that would normally have me very frazzled, but having started my morning on a positive note, I found it much easier not to sweat all the small, irritating things. So thank you."

☞ When you think back on some of the "worst" things that have ever happened to you, it might be true that if these things had not happened, your life would be different from what it is today. If things in your life have improved since then, give recognition for those lessons and the "teachers" that pushed you to where you are.

📖 Consistency is the key for a gratitude journal. Write every day, even if you only have time for a sentence or two. When you're having a bad day, page back through and look at all the things you've written down. It's an immediate pick-me-up. If you miss a day, don't knock yourself; just begin again. It is important to transcribe your blessings. After all, when you compose, you are utilizing many more senses than just thinking. You FEEL the pen in your hand, you HEAR the scratching of your pen and the rustling of the pages, you SEE the words on paper, and you EXPERIENCE the emotion of grace. Recording thankfulness gives it power.

Dr. Robert Emmons shares tips for generating the utmost psychological rewards from your journaling:

- **Make the decision** to become happier as a result of your journaling. Even if you don't necessarily believe you're going to notice a difference, create an intention of pleasure from your practice.

- **Add details** about the particular person or event for which you are grateful instead of just making a list of items. It can get boring if you just write down a list of words.

- **Focus more on the people** to whom you are grateful rather than material objects. We can get "stuff" any time; it's the people in our lives that make it magical.

- **Try subtraction instead of addition.** Imagine what your life would be like if you did not have certain blessings in your life. Think about George Baily in "It's a Wonderful Life" and think about how your life would be if you did not have these things.

- **Enjoy the unexpected events** that give you pleasure. Make a point to savor your surprises. As you look for and appreciate what you have, chances are good you'll receive even more for which to be thankful.

- **Don't beat yourself up** if you miss a day. Get yourself back into the habit and enjoy the time you spend expressing contentment with your life.

Because my gratitude list is composed in the morning, I wanted to find something positive that could be done in the evening. Watching the news is not an option - planting stories of murder and mayhem into my subconscious before going to sleep is certainly not productive. After all, if something bad enough happens, someone is going to tell me about it anyway, so why waste the time? (And, believe me, when something bad happens, everyone wants to talk about it.)

In order to incorporate thankfulness into my evening ritual, I created an exercise called "The ABC's of Gratitude." Drifting off to sleep, I choose a random letter in the alphabet and think about something to be grateful for that begins with that letter. Then, I go to the next letter, and so on. For example, "I am grateful for my BROTHER and the heart-to-heart conversation we had today"; "I am grateful for my CALENDAR filling up with speaking gigs"; "I am grateful for my DAD and the way he tells me he loves me when he can't find the words to say anything else."

It generally takes about six letters before I fall fast asleep. This is why I no longer start with "A"—I never made it past "F!" As a former insomniac, this is a drug-free way to fill my mind with positivity and drift off to a sound, peaceful sleep.

The advantage of journaling in the evening is that you can reflect back on your day in an affirmative way. Before you go to bed, write down 3-5 things that happened during the day for which you are grateful. Get into the feeling and relive your happiest moments. If you had a bad experience, see if you can find just one or two things about that incident which you can count as a blessing. In a worst-case scenario, be thankful for the lessons learned and appreciate that today is now over and tomorrow is a brand new day.

The power of the gratitude journal is indisputable. I have heard countless stories—both in my research and from attendees in my workshops. Sam shared with me that she had been struggling in her relationship with her mother for years and she was not look-ing forward to her mom's holiday visit. One evening, as Sam was writing in her journal, her mother walked in and asked what she was writing. Sam decided to take the first step and share with her mom how grateful she was to have her mother in her life and for the opportunity to have them there with Sam and her family for the holidays. Sam says, "After that conversation, for the rest of the visit, my mother never once criticized me. The rest of the visit was joyful and easy. No longer will I have to dread her visit."

☞ Even if you're not quite there yet in believing that this will make a difference, accept my **30-day Challenge**. Simply write down 3-5 things that you appreciate at some point each day. At the end of thirty days, see how you feel. If you feel great, keep it up. If you're not feeling any different, pay attention to your general mood after you discontinue the habit. You may not notice any dramatic changes right away, but you'll find you feel better when you invest the time to be thankful.

The top five things I am grateful for today are:

_____

_____

_____

_____

_____

_____

SELF

"Life without thankfulness is devoid of love and passion.
Hope without thankfulness is lacking in fine perception.
Faith without thankfulness lacks strength and fortitude.
Every virtue divorced from thankfulness is maimed and
limps along the spiritual road."
– John Henry Jowett

In conducting research on the effect of gratitude on people's lives, I did a little "crowd sourcing" on a social media site. I posted the question: "How do you incorporate gratitude and appreciation into your business?" Now, you have to agree that it's a pretty innocent question, right? As with many previously published questions, I expected the usual vanilla responses. Imagine my surprise when the very first answer was: "You don't need to incorporate gratitude and appreciation into your business because people are just going to take advantage of you anyway."

Wow, I thought, here was someone who must have been hurt in the past and was still pretty bitter about it. Taking a deep breath, I replied, "I'm sorry that you feel that way." She countered with: "That's okay, I'm a big girl now and I'm moving on." Deciding on a bold move, I proposed that she take my 30-day Challenge. She was to write down 3-5 things she appreciated in her life every day for thirty days and then update me with her progress. I was pleasantly surprised when she e-mailed me back with a completely changed tone, saying, "Thank you for being so positive, I will do that right away." Sometimes, all it takes it a little kindness and attention to help someone make a change.

We corresponded over the next couple weeks, and when thirty days were up, I asked her how it was going. She replied, "I really haven't been feeling that much difference, but I went on vacation and **other people noticed**." It didn't matter that she did not believe that this would work for her. It did not matter that she did not feel any differently. The only thing that mattered was that she took a minute or two every day to appreciate something in her life, and her attitude noticeably changed.

After one of my Grategy® seminars, a woman approached me. She said that she had been keeping a gratitude journal for the last three months. She hadn't noticed anything remarkable in her life and considered giving it up. However, on the very day she was going to quit, her husband commented to her, "There's something different about you lately. I don't know what it is, but you seem a lot happier." Needless to say, she decided to continue with her routine.

When we set out to try something new, our own transformation often happens gradually. We don't necessarily notice the changes that are starting to take place - but others will.

My husband underwent a similar response when I began my journal. Although he had no idea about my daily chronicling, he started offering more verbal acknowledgment for the little things I did. Because he was thanking me, I began reciprocating in kind. It became a virtuous circle and our marriage has grown as a result. (The relationship section of this book will show you more ways to positively impact your connection with your spouse or significant other.) The positive energy that surrounds my daily musings enables Scott to be more supportive of me and my entrepreneurial adventures. Being thankful creates a vibrancy that permeates everyone and everything we come into contact with.

Have you ever met individuals whose general lack of gratefulness sucks the very soul out of the space they inhabit? On several occasions I've had coffee with "Karen," a woman going through a very difficult period in her life. She was drowning in self-pity and could not see her way out of it. Listening intently to her plight, I shared one of my favorite books by Dr. John Demartini titled, *Count Your Blessings: The Healing Power of Gratitude and Love.* I then suggested she attempt a gratitude journal to see how it worked. Karen left the coffee shop inspired and happy, promising that she was going to get started immediately.

Sadly, a few months later, when we met for coffee again the get-together mirrored our first encounter. Still stuck in the muck, Karen complained bitterly about her life. After asking if she had instituted her gratitude journal, she emphatically professed that she had "nothing to be thankful for." Although we discussed the fact that she woke up in a bed, had a house with electricity, and could walk down the stairs unassisted, she was unable or unwilling to accept that she had a LOT to marvel at. Her reluctance to experience life in a new way not only affected her outlook, it shaped all of her relationships as well. After all, who wants to associate with such a negative Nelly? Hopefully, in time, Karen will reach a point where staying the same is more painful than changing. It will be at that instance when metamorphosis will take place.

If Karen had actually taken the promised time each day to get to a place of gratitude, she may have experienced a story like Sam's. After hearing about the power of a gratitude journal at a Grategy® event, Sam decided to give it a whirl to see what kind of difference it would make in her life. "My gratitude journal helped me see all the wonderful people in my life. I knew that I had acquaintances. Being truly grateful for my friends this past year has led me to some very rewarding, deep friendships that have blessed me in so many ways." When we start with what we already have, we'll often discover that we have so much more than we originally thought-a wonderful blessing in itself.

☞ Think of someone in your life who whom you have a challenging relationship. Now imagine the character traits they possess which you appreciate. Dig deep if you need to and start with one or two positive attributes. Once you get started, add to the list.

_____

_____

_____

_____

_____

_____

_____

_____

_____

_____

_____

_____

_____

_____

_____

_____

_____

_____

_____

_____

_____

SELF

"What lies behind us and what lies before us are tiny matters compared to what lies within us."
— **Ralph Waldo Emerson**

As in life, anything worth doing probably involves work. Advice columnist Ann Landers once said, "Opportunities are usually disguised as hard work, so most people don't recognize them." Sometimes it's easy to give thanks, sometimes it's not. We have to be willing to do whatever is necessary to appreciate what we have – even if we have to make stuff up along the way.

Your mind does not recognize a truth from a "lie," and if you tell yourself something often enough, you begin to believe it. When you imagine your life the way you desire it, are grateful for the things you have, and write down or visualize your blessings repeatedly, you plant the seed of positive intention. Your subconscious will then begin to activate a plan for the achievement of your dreams and you are on your way.

We've already discussed how a gratitude journal is a powerful tool to harness the power of appreciation. The consistent contemplation of the goodness in our lives helps us create opportunities that we may have missed if we weren't paying attention.

In my Grategy® workshops I ask, "How many of you keep a gratitude journal?" Although the numbers are starting to climb, a high percentage of people still do not practice regularly. Attendees tell me, "Well, I'm a naturally grateful person; I'm thankful all the time." That's a wonderful character trait to have. If you're one of these people, why not take the challenge and keep an appreciation diary of those thoughts. Because you're using so many more senses while writing them, than when you're just thinking them; the positive effects are multiplied.

Others in my classes have confessed, "I used to keep a gratitude journal, but I've stopped writing in it. I probably need to get back into the habit of doing it again." Upon probing further, many of them admit they felt a lot better about their lives when they were recording their gratitude.

Isn't it funny that when we find something that works, something that makes us feel good, we stop doing it? Why does this happen? Sometimes we take for granted all the good in our lives. Perhaps we get distracted by "putting out fires" and we don't devote our time to appreciation. If you're one of the people who used to keep a journal, make a commitment to yourself to begin again. It's a powerful habit.

Greg learned about the power of giving thanks at a workshop that taught "The Practice" – a combination of yoga and several other elements that begins and ends with appreciation. Greg explains, "In 'The Practice', it begins by stating three things you are grateful for and ends the same way. I still do it every morning. Starting the day with gratitude changes your thinking and helps you to look at the world differently. We begin thinking in terms of plenty instead of lack. Maybe because we think in terms of what we already have that we are grateful for and we begin to realize how much we have to be grateful for. This isn't just financial plenty - it is plenty in terms of love, relationships and other areas of life. In my own life I have seen the difference."

A regular practice of gratefulness does help to strengthen that all-important gratitude muscle. Remember when we talked about the fact that, "gratitude is not for wimps"? Here's Christine's story about how her innate sense of appreciation helped her through her dad's death.

Christine's father died in 1998. "When I was growing up, my dad called me his 'yard bird' because I helped him with outside chores: shoveling snow in winter, cleaning up the yard in spring, maintaining the flowers and lawn in summer, and raking leaves in fall. On one particular day after my dad had passed, I sat alone, feeling sad and missing him – his distinctive laugh, robust bear hugs, and unconditional love. I thought I had lost him forever.

"Suddenly I began thinking about the many natural talents that I had inherited from him, like his incredible sense of direction, his savvy bargain-hunting skills, and his love of the outdoors. I realized at that moment that because his DNA lives within me, I carry him with me wherever I go. The thought comforted me.

"My gratitude cup overflowed that day, reminding me that by being grateful for my father, I was also grateful for the person I have become."

By being able to achieve gratefulness, Christine found a new strength within herself. She could easily access her father's presence whenever she wanted to be close to him, and she could pride herself on the talents she inherited from him that made her life more fulfilling.

When we consider the benefits of gratitude in terms of our outlook on life, doesn't it make sense to make it a habit? You bring forth an energy, and your perspective will change. When you are conscious of the world around you and your place in it, it's easy to recognize your blessings.

☞ If you haven't done it yet, start your gratitude journal now. Look for those precious few moments to meditate on throughout your day and experience life to the fullest. Just a couple minutes each day can be transformative.

I am starting my gratitude journal on (date):_____

In the next chapter, we'll look at the physical and mental health benefits of practicing gratitude.

Notes:

_____

_____

_____

_____

_____

_____

_____

_____

_____

_____

_____

_____

_____

_____

_____

_____

_____

_____

_____

_____

Chapter 2

Health

The Healthy Habits of Highly Thankful People

"Gratitude is the miracle cure for every moment of disease. It's the fastest way to dissolve anxiety, to heal disappointment, to replace negativity with positivity. It is the connecting energy to God."
— **Neal Donald Walsch**

Gratitude not only feels good, it's good medicine—literally. Many research projects have focused on the science of being thankful and its effect on psychological, emotional, and physical well-being. When individuals consistently cherish what they have, they experience more optimism, happiness, and stronger relationships than those who do not. Grateful people are also less likely to suffer from depression, alcoholism, envy, or greed.

When Colleen was diagnosed with a brain tumor, she learned the value of choosing positivity over negativity. Her tumor was benign, but because it pressed up against her brainstem, it had to be removed. She had it eradicated and subsequently struggled with depression and unhappiness. When she finally became "sick and tired of being sick and tired," she made a conscious choice to give thanks for her experience. After all, she had faced her own mortality and won. She stepped back, conducted a self-assessment and realized how incredibly blessed she was. Now, whenever she finds herself dealing with other medical or financial issues, she finds a way back to gratitude. She says, "I feel really lucky."

Chris has always been one of the most optimistic people I know. She is the woman who introduced me to positive thinking in the late 1980s, and for that I am indebted to her. Chris shared her incredible story of gratitude when she faced her son's health challenge. It's an extraordinary story of love and healing which demonstrates the full force of a positive mental attitude.

When her 25-year-old son Christopher was diagnosed with Non-Hodgkin's lymphoma, Chris decided that even though the doctors gave him a very low chance for survival, she would make sure that through visualization techniques and positive thinking her son would pull through. She never gave him the opportunity to believe anything but a complete cure for his illness.

Chris was only allowed to visit her son for 15 minutes twice a day. She took full advantage of their time together to inspire him to get better. She held Christopher's hand, telling him to visualize summer with the warm weather, the sun, and the flowers that he loved. She noticed that every time she was with him, a certain light came on and a beep sounded on the equipment he was hooked up to. The nurse told her that it indicated that Christopher was breathing on his own. She knew she was making progress.

"Christopher recovered enough to come home for the summer, still on chemotherapy, with short stays back at the Clinic. Together, we listened to tapes, we talked about the future, we concentrated on the beauty of every moment. By December, he was in total remission. They called it a miracle."

Christopher elected to go through a bone marrow transplant as a preventative measure. He has now been in remission for over 20 years. Chris is grateful for her son and truly appreciates the "miracle" of positive thought which saved him.

This was not an isolated incident. The University of North Carolina studied the interactions between cancer patients and their support groups. Researcher Sara Algoe found that when acts of gratitude were included, the positive effects lasted well over a month. She saw that giving thanks is a potent emotion that feeds on itself—a vicious circle that is anything but vicious. "It must be really powerful," Algoe commented.

We cope with the tragedies that happen to us and our loved ones by keeping a sense of optimism. This allows us to feel hope and provides time to adjust to unexpected circumstances. Having a conscious awareness of the blessings in our lives fosters the strength to endure any hardships.

Many times people who face an affliction feel isolated. They believe they have to put on a "happy face" so their loved ones do not feel uncomfortable. A true friend has the courage to step into the loved one's shoes so he or she doesn't feel alone. Psychologist Lynn Margolies, PhD, reminds us, "Before you tell someone stricken by tragedy how lucky they are, take a moment to consider whether you would want to trade places so you could be the 'lucky' one."

Bill didn't feel so "lucky" when he was diagnosed with skin cancer. His dermatologist noticed a small spot on the left side of his face that she thought didn't look right. She had it biopsied and the results came back positive for melanoma. Bill was set up with a surgeon immediately, and after four facial surgeries, Bill is cancer-free and did not have to go through chemo or radiation therapy.

Throughout his ordeal, Bill found much to give thanks for: "I am grateful for having a wife who stands beside me regardless. Of having the opportunity of seeking four second-opinions and finally selecting a doctor who did a magnificent job of cutting open half my face but leaving no trace. I am grateful for friends who prayed for us while this was going on and gave us a tremendous amount of moral support."

Because Bill's positive attitude showed up in all areas of his life, he successfully battled this health challenge. He learned his lesson and gladly shared his experience. He wants to impart this tip: "Although I had a great experience, I don't recommend cancer to anyone. Wear SUNBLOCK!!!"

From time to time, life throws us a curve ball, but we still have a choice. Like Colleen, we can initially opt to suffer from depression and unhappiness before realizing our many blessings. Or, like Chris and Bill, we can decide that our illness isn't going to stand a fighting chance, as long as we have some say in the matter.

☞ Do what you can, with what you have, where you are. If you are currently facing a health challenge, write down anything that you can be grateful for in your situation. Refer to this list whenever you need a pick-me-up.

_____

_____

_____

_____

_____

_____

_____

_____

HEALTH

"If you have health, you probably will be happy, and if you have health and happiness, you have all the wealth you need, even if it is not all you want."
— **Elbert Hubbard**

When we suffer from a disease, we often get caught up in the "I don't feel well" syndrome. Looking for ways to feel grateful instead of ill will make you feel better all around. A study conducted by Drs. Robert Emmons and Michael McCullough examined the impact of gratitude on a group of people battling various neuromuscular complications. They found that the participants who kept daily appreciation logs were more satisfied with their lives and were more optimistic about their future than the group who did not.

Jori Reijonen, Ph.D., has a neuromuscular disease called Charcot Marie Tooth (CMT). She writes, "As I have dealt with my diagnosis and symptoms of neuromuscular disease over the past few years, sometimes my emotions have given way to worry or despair. My thoughts have turned to questions such as, 'Why me?', 'What will happen to me?', and 'How will I be able to take care of my family, my work, my rating, my volunteer work, etc., if I can't walk or can't use my hands?' When I begin to despair, one of my most useful tools is prayer, often in the form of keeping a gratitude journal.

"When I take time to focus on the many blessings in my life, I turn my attention away from my physical complaints and on to the many blessings I experience every day. The act of putting these blessings onto paper makes them tangible. If my thoughts are too dark to begin writing, I can prompt myself by reading previous entries that helps put me into the right frame of mind to begin to consider the many blessings in my life, all that I have for which to be thankful.

"Keeping track of my blessings during good times comes easily. To challenge myself, I look for the good, for why I should be grateful, even in circumstances that appear completely negative, such as my diagnosis with Charcot Marie Tooth. It turns out that many positives can be found, even related to my health difficulties.

"Here's my gratitude list related to my diagnosis of CMT: I can still walk and use my hands; good adaptive devices to help me; relative mildness and a recent slowing of progression in my CMT; excellent medical care; becoming involved with the MDA and CMTA; the amazing people I have met; reaching out to others with CMT through starting a support group; reaching out to others through my writing; increased self-awareness; gains in emotional strength and resilience; increased empathy for others; spiritual growth.

"It turns out there have been so many blessings that have come out of this diagnosis. Focusing on those blessings improves my mood and gives me strength. Gratitude journaling remains one of the best tools that I know of for promoting happiness and emotional strength."

Jori's gratitude diary has made a difference in her life, and she has made it her mission to support others in similar circumstances by serving as BellaOnline's Neuromuscular Diseases Editor. Her readers have shared their stories and her emphasis on appreciation is helping others to do the same for themselves.

In addition to its effect on neuromuscular diseases, other studies have shown how a thankful approach can support heart health. Researchers at the University of Connecticut have discovered that being appreciative can protect against heart attacks. They revealed that people who suffered a heart attack and subsequently realized the benefits of the attack – such as valuing loved ones and their life in general – experienced a lower risk of a recurrence.

Rich "celebrated" his thirtieth wedding anniversary by having a heart attack. Waking up around 6:00am, his chest felt heavy, as if a four-year-old was sitting on him. He thought that maybe he had just slept wrong and developed a kink in his back. He showered and lay on the living room floor to see if he could straighten it out but it didn't help.

He recalled the mnemonic device the Boy Scouts developed for recognizing a heart attack, which consisted of shortness of breath, unusual sweating, etc. He didn't have any other symptoms other than chest pressure, so he went downstairs to check out his symptoms on the internet. One of the websites advised calling 9-1-1 right away if one experienced any symptoms; after all, it's better to be safe than sorry.

He dialed 9-1-1 and the paramedics soon arrived. They asked a lot of questions and took his vital signs. Initially, the paramedics did not believe it to be a heart attack. They gave Rich some nitroglycerine spray to help control any arrhythmias that might be causing the heaviness and loaded him up in the ambulance.

Things started to change once they arrived at the hospital. The ambulance tech said that the EKG looked very different from what he saw at the house. A nurse arrived and shaved Rich's groin area. They took him up to the operating room to put a stent into the artery where he had the blockage.

In his words, he was "very glad I didn't ignore it and have this escalate while I was driving to pick up Mom or on our way down to Madison." He was very thankful he did not disregard his symptoms, and his only thoughts were those of being able to go home and give his wife and son a big hug.

THE UPSIDE OF DOWN TIMES

Rich's positive attitude will help prevent future episodes. He radiates appreciation for the life he has, and now he's thankful that he'll be able to continue on and be there for his wife and son.

Even if your health is not where you want it to be, treasure the health you have. Give thanks for your sight and the education that allows you to read this book. Yes! Be grateful for the use of your limbs and functioning fingers to turn the pages. Remember, do what you can with what you have wherever you are. There is always going to be someone in worse shape than you are – counting your blessings for your health will help improve your attitude and well-being.

If you are hale and hearty, **never** take it for granted. It's been said that we spend the first part of our lives using our health to get wealth and the second part of our life using our wealth to get our health. Appreciate the fact that you are fit and chances are good that you can get through any challenges that show up later on in life.

Take a moment to consider what you value about your health? Spend a couple moments and FEEL health and wellness coursing through your veins, uplifting your energy and vitality. (If you're not quite there, imagine how you would feel IF health and wellness were coursing through your body.) How do you feel now?

_____

_____

_____

_____

_____

_____

_____

HEALTH

"Holding onto anger is like grasping onto a hot coal with the intent of throwing it at someone else. You are the one who gets burned."
– Buddha

The Institute of HeartMath is an internationally renowned non-profit organization that has conducted extensive research on the relationship between the heart and various emotions. One study compared the effects of frustration and appreciation on the performance of the heart by subjecting a random group of people to a period of irritation and then examining their heart rate variability (the interval between heart beats). The resulting pattern appeared uneven and jagged (imagine a lie detector test when the person is lying). They took that same group of people and changed their emotion to one of appreciation. The heart rate now presented as smooth and even - a noticeably calmer pattern.

This is one of the many studies that illustrate the physical benefits of choosing to feel positive emotions. We decide how we are going to respond to any given situation, and when we react optimistically, we help our hearts become stronger and healthier.

HeartMath also compared the effects of compassion and anger on the immune system. They discovered that when a person experiences five minutes of anger, it suppresses the immune system for up to six hours. Those same five minutes spent in compassion increases the efficiency of the immune system for up to six hours.

One example of this pattern to which almost everyone can relate is driving. Think about it: you're driving to work and some "jerk" cuts you off. At this point, you have a couple choices. Negative responses include: speeding up and tailgating the inconsiderate individual, pulling up alongside the car to glare or (obscenely) gesture, or racing ahead and returning the favor. Select any of the above and you carry that negativity with you when you get to the office.

At the office you moan and complain about your road rage incident to everyone in immediate proximity. You swap stories with your co-workers about all of the jerks who have ever cut you off. When you start trading Highway Jerk stories, you're spreading all those negative vibes to others. It's like a ripple of misery. Your mood progressively worsens, your energy plummets, and, if you do this repeatedly, people avoid you.

Let's rewind. Instead of flying into a rage, say you choose to imagine that the "jerk" has just received word that a loved one was in an accident and is rushing to the hospital to be by this person's side. You feel compassion, maybe offering a prayer for whatever is going on in his or her life.

By taking this action instead, you activate good feelings because you underwent an anonymous feeling of kindness—after all, that person will never be aware of the fact that you sent a positive vibe. You release any frustration that you may have initially felt and go about the rest of your day. It's over, and you no longer have to think about it or carry it with you. Big difference, huh? Those five minutes of blessing and release have a much bigger impact on your immune system and overall health than you realize.

When we pick compassion over anger, we strengthen our immune system. Here's something else to consider in the course of keeping ourselves fit. All our lives we have heard of the importance of washing our hands to prevent colds and flu. As a matter of fact, when I was in medical sales, I presented more than 300 continuing education classes on hand hygiene.

One of the studies referenced in this class was by a researcher who interviewed his healthcare staff to see what percentage of the time they washed their hands in accordance with industry requirements. Eighty-five percent of the people claimed that they always washed their hands when mandated. When asked about their co-workers, they reported that they thought that their peers washed their hands about 50% of the time when necessary. However, the researcher's unidentifiable observer found that his staff actually washed their hands only 26% of the time when mandated. (Makes you want to stay away from hospitals, doesn't it?)

So what exactly does this have to do with being thankful? I believe that if you asked people if they are grateful on a regular basis, most of them will say, "Oh yes, definitely. I am always appreciative of what I have." If you ask them about how grateful they feel other people are, they will probably give it about a 50/50 chance. However, if you followed them around for the day and observed how many times they acknowledged others, verbally expressed appreciation, and reflected a positive attitude, the actual numbers may vary greatly from the original report. Food for thought: how's your gratitude hygiene?

Whether we are currently dealing with challenges or are blessed with overall healthiness, we can enhance our current state by choosing positive emotions over negative thoughts. When we decide to make better emotional choices, we improve our attitude, our vitality, our mental AND our physical well-being. Bottom line: opting for optimism is always healthy.

THE UPSIDE OF DOWN TIMES

☞ What can you do to ensure that you choose positive emotions, i.e. compassion over anger or gratitude over frustration? Think about your habitual negative reactions and begin to choose more effective ways to respond.

I can choose these positive emotions instead:

_____

_____

_____

_____

_____

_____

_____

_____

_____

_____

_____

_____

_____

_____

_____

_____

_____

_____

_____

_____

_____

_____

_____

HEALTH

"I expect to pass through life but once. If, therefore, there by any kindness I can show or any good thing I can do to any fellow being, let me do it now and not defer to neglect it, as I shall not pass this way again."
— **William Penn**

We show gratitude for the good in our lives by volunteering to help others. "Individuals who do volunteer work sometimes speak of the benefits they receive from service," writes Dr. Robert Emmons in his book *Thanks!* "Since service to others helped them to find their own inner spirituality, they were grateful for the opportunity to serve."

Recently divorced and facing the holidays alone in December 1984, Cleveland advertising executive, Dick Clough, filled up his Mustang convertible with plush toys and handed them out to patients and family members at St. Vincent Charity Medical Center in downtown Cleveland. Having related the positive experience with clients and friends, the following year Clough traded the Mustang for a city bus, added several more hospitals to the itinerary, and took a whole crew of "elves" on what was then called "Santa's Express."

Seven years later following Dick's decision to address a chronic battle with substance abuse, he refocused the project on needy kids, and homeless men, women, children and families.

In December 2011, the project celebrated its 27th anniversary, and evolved into literally a "Tour of Good Cheer" with two sixty-passenger tour buses (one for elves, and one for merchandise). Clough and his merry band of forty-five friends distributed nearly 5,000 pieces of clothing, blankets, backpacks, toys, and more.

THE UPSIDE OF DOWN TIMES

The ten hour bus Tour encompasses nine facilities with a total population exceeding 850 adults and children. The week before Christmas, (Santa) Clough distributes additional merchandise to the local Ronald McDonald House, an orphanage, and several half-way programs.

Dick works on the Tour year-around, and intensively from mid-November to the Tour date a week before Christmas. The warm feeling from giving to those in need, and affording his many friends and colleagues the opportunity to experience the same lasts for months. And just as the glow begins to fade, the organizing pace picks up in preparation of the next Tour of Good Cheer. In so many ways, the project defines my friend Dick Clough.

I have first-hand experience with the Tour, and have witnessed the difference that it makes. People on the tour kindly acknowledge those whom they bring coats, sweaters, and others gifts. Dick and his elves go the extra mile in making the recipient feel special, letting each know that we care about making the holiday season a little brighter. It's a magical night for the recipients, who receive the warmth of the clothing as well as the warmth in which they are treated. It's also a miraculous night for all the volunteers on the tour, and the energy is palatable. Even after almost twelve hours of work, the liveliness and spirit aboard our bus is still going strong.

Volunteering does not have to equal the size and scope of the Tour of Good Cheer. Studies show that people who participate in any kind of volunteer work on a regular basis experience lower mortality rates, greater functional ability, and lower rates of depression later in life than those who do not. Plus, older volunteers receive the greatest benefits because it gives them a sense of purpose at a time when their roles are changing.

However, giving of your time, talent, or treasure at any age vastly pays off in knowing that your contribution has potentially changed someone's life for the better. When we come to realize the number of people who are less fortunate than we are, we learn that we can serve others and ourselves in the process.

Volunteers give their time without expecting any form of compensation. They have the intent of assisting others; however, common wisdom suggests that those who give of themselves also receive many benefits in return, including the positive feeling referred to as "helper's high," increased trust in others, and increased social and political participation.

My brother, Scott, has a successful podiatry practice. Because of his passion and desire to help others, he is enthusiastic about giving back. He not only donates his time at the local free clinic, he provides free medical care to his patients without insurance. While his service comes at no charge, there is a catch: he requires his patient to "pay it forward" and do something nice for someone else.

Scott shares the story of one gentleman with a serious foot infection who did not have the money or the insurance to pay for it. After letting him know about the "pay it forward" stipulation, Scott agreed to remedy the infection. A few weeks after the successful treatment, the patient came into the office to let Scott know that he had stopped to assist a woman on the freeway with a flat tire the previous day – something he had never done before. The patient was radiant as he felt the sheer joy of helping someone with no expectation of return. Scott felt great because he knew that he had made a difference not only in this man's health, but in his life as well.

THE UPSIDE OF DOWN TIMES

There are numerous benefits to volunteering, and once again, research supports it. In a report titled the "United Healthcare/ Volunteer Match: Do Good. Live Well Survey," people who volunteer not only enhanced their physical and mental health, but strengthened their relationships at work as well.

Some of the key findings include:

- More than 68% of those who volunteered in the past year reported that it made them feel physically healthier.

- 29% of volunteers who suffered from a chronic condition say that it has helped them manage their chronic illness.

- 89% of volunteers agree that offering their time improved their sense of well-being.

- 73% of volunteers feel that it lowered their stress levels.

- 92% of volunteers agree that helping out enriches their sense of purpose in life.

- More than three-quarters of volunteers who participate in service activities through work report feeling better about their employer because of the employer's involvement in their volunteer activities.

Harnessing the power of appreciation involves stepping out of your comfort zone. In our busy lives, it's not always easy to find the time to devote to helping someone else. There may be discomfort in dealing with the needy and the physically or mentally disabled.

HEALTH

However, when we can stretch ourselves to do something for someone else, we make this world a better place to live.

☞ What can you do today to "pay it forward" and help someone else? Keep the details of your activities to yourself. You'll bask in the anonymity of your good deeds.

_____

_____

_____

_____

_____

_____

_____

_____

_____

_____

_____

_____

_____

_____

_____

_____

_____

_____

_____

_____

_____

_____

_____

_____

Chapter 3

Others

How to Thank Friends and Appreciate People

*"Hope sees the invisible, feels the intangible and
achieves the impossible."*
– Charles Caleb

Think about all the people passing through your life on a daily basis who are basically "invisible" to you. You don't see them, you don't acknowledge them; in fact, you barely know they exist. How would your day change if you took a moment to acknowledge these individuals? What about the person at the coffee shop that you regularly patronize on your way to work? You walk in, bleary-eyed from a very short night of sleep. You order your non-fat, café mocha and grumpily wait for it to be handed to you. When it finally arrives, you take a big swig, anticipating it coursing through your veins – now you are ready to tackle the day.

But, what if, instead of the usual routine, you go into the coffee shop, make eye contact with the barista, manage a big smile and remark, "How can you be so chipper at this time in the morning?"

"Ugh," you may be thinking, "I can barely open my eyes before I get my caffeine fix, and now you want me to be NICE too?!!!"

OTHERS

Yes, I do.

Look for people with whom you have regular contact but have made little to no effort to acknowledge, such as the mail carrier or the janitor of your building. When you take the time to observe these individuals, you'll see how many of them walk with a slouch, don't make eye contact, and don't expect to be recognized because, for the most part, they're not. Countless people feel that they work hard, and yet nobody is even aware of their existence. It's time to change the pattern of overlooking others—for your own benefit as well as theirs.

In any cases, a sense of connection is missing from our communications. We need to look for ways to re-establish lost bonds, as well as create new relationships. A smile, a nod, making friendly eye contact   it doesn't take a lot of effort, but it can mean the world to someone else.

Ann discovered the benefits of creating a new relationship by ac-knowledging another while at a training seminar. Walking down the hall to a breakout session, she happened to smile and say hello to Richard. That brief encounter led to a conversation and a fast friendship. As it turned out, Richard was able to offer Ann invaluable support, which benefited her tremendously with her business. Ann shares, "You can either choose to ignore people or you can look at them in the eye and say, "Hi." And, that's just what we did, and that started the conversation. You know it's just putting a smile on somebody's face can completely change your life."

Here's one way to start the habit: the next time you are home when the UPS driver comes around, greet him or her at the door with a smile and thank the person for being so conscientious when delivering your package. Are your boxes always covered to keep them from getting wet in the rain? Let your driver know you appreciate the extra effort. Those men and women toil for long hours, and much of the time they don't get the opportunity to connect with people - just boxes. Take a moment and say, "Thanks." Chances are, you will cause a ripple effect: The driver will be more inclined to treat the next customers with diligent consideration, and your driver will surely take care of you the next time around. It's a true win-win situation.

When I was in medical sales, one of my clients was located in a large medical campus in the heart of the city. In order to get from the parking garage to the main entrance, you had to wait for a crossing guard to let you cross the street. Imagine this scenario: It was 6:30am in early February, completely dark, 18°F, and the wintry winds gusted at about twenty miles per hour. A group of adults impatiently waited for the light to change so they can rush inside to the welcoming warmth of the building. The traffic light finally changed, and every one of those adults walked by the guard either scowling or ignoring him.

When it was my turn to cross, I looked the guard in the eyes as I passed him, patted him on the shoulder, grinned, and said, "Dude, I am so glad I'm not you today!" He LIT up. A huge smile crossed his face, and he clearly appeared happier than he was just a few seconds ago. Why? Because he felt acknowledged; for a moment, someone else mentally traded places with him and felt what it was like to be in his shoes. All of us crossing the street would be warm and cozy in just a few minutes while this guard probably had several more hours of biting cold and ill-tempered adults to deal with. It took two seconds of effort for a huge payoff—for both him and me. Even though this event happened several years ago, I still feel the warmth of our "moment."

OTHERS

Mary Beth showed her girls the true meaning of Christmas as well as the value of appreciating others in her story. "When my girls were small, I used to take them out to see the Christmas lights on the houses. They would 'ooh' and 'ahh' at the pretty lights and decorations. I kept thinking that people do this for the benefit of others, spending their time and money to make it nice for the rest of us to enjoy. I got the idea of sending thank you notes to the five best houses, according to the girls. So, they kept busy making cards out of old cut up Christmas cards, pictures from magazines, and hand-drawn renditions of the houses. We then went around and put them in their mailboxes.

"My older daughter, who had signed her full name on her creations, got a phone call one night. The lucky recipients of one of her masterpieces had called every Sammon in the phone book looking for her, so they could personally thank her for the picture, telling her NO ONE had EVER thanked them for their Christmas display in their yard. They liked the picture SO MUCH, that they framed it and put it on their mantle! Lauren was THRILLED. We kept this tradition up until the girls lost interest in driving around looking at lights with me!"

At a recent seminar, Colin Powell shared stories from his time in the White House. Along with the glitz and glamour of the job, travels to exotic places, and accommodations that few of us can even imagine, he imparts a simple story about the woman who took care of cleaning his office. He talked about the loving care she extended to make sure that everything was perfect for him. He deeply appreciated the work she did and he let her know it. On a regular basis he would tell her, "I do my job as well as I do because you do your job as well as you do."

THE UPSIDE OF DOWN TIMES

No matter what your political leanings, you can probably agree that in his tenure, Colin Powell was one of the most powerful men on the planet. Picture for a moment what it would be like to be his cleaning person and hear the heartfelt words from such an influential man. Would you ever leave his employ, even for more money to go elsewhere? Probably not. We work harder for recognition and appreciation than we will ever work for money.

☞ Who in your life is "invisible" to you? When you go out to lunch, do you ignore or kindly acknowledge the server by name? Have you made eye contact with the clerk at the grocery store and asked him or her how their day is going? Today, make it a point to "see" everyone you come into contact with. Something as small as a smile, a nod or a friendly greeting will go a long way in making someone else's day a little brighter.

When I "saw" people today, it made me realize:

_____

_____

_____

_____

_____

_____

_____

_____

_____

_____

_____

_____

OTHERS

"To laugh often and much; to win the respect of intelligent people and the affection of children...to leave the world a better place...to know even one life has breathed easier because you have lived. This is to have succeeded."
– Ralph Waldo Emerson

In families that encourage a spirit of appreciation, a favorable impact has also been recorded by researchers. When kids value what they have, they tend to be less materialistic, achieve better grades, and set higher goals. Their health is also better, with fewer headaches and stomachaches. President Abraham Lincoln once said, "There is but one way to teach a child the way he should go, and that is to travel that way yourself." When children see their parents modeling appreciative behavior, they are more likely to pick up on it, too.

"A lot of these findings are things we learned in kindergarten or our grandmothers told us, but we now have scientific evidence to prove them," says Dr. Jeffrey J. Froh, an assistant professor of psychology at Hofstra University in Hempstead, N.Y., who has conducted much research with children.

Similar to Dr. Emmons research with adults, Drs. Jeffrey Froh and William Sefick pioneered gratitude research, with children, to see if there was any difference. In 2008, they followed 221 middle school students for five weeks, randomly assigning students to one of the three conditions: gratitude, hassles, and a control group. The gratitude group wrote down things for which they were grateful, the hassles group recollected all of the annoyances and the control group simply recorded the day's events without emotion.

The results were identical to the adult studies. In the gratitude group, the researchers found higher levels of optimism, increased life satisfaction, and decreased negative feeling. The results were still occurring three weeks after the study was complete.

Froh states, "I don't mean to suggest that counting their blessings for two weeks will cause adolescents to stock up on thank you cards; I think becoming a grateful person takes a prolonged, consistent effort. But, the time to start practicing gratitude is when you're young, and I think schools can play a vital role—especially since our intervention only took a few minutes a day. As our results suggest, gratitude serves the school's educational mission while also tending to students' social and emotional needs. By helping to teach it, we might make kids more receptive to everything else they can learn from their teachers, parents, and friends."

Starting gratitude at a young age can be easy and fun. When children learn to speak and ask for something, have them say, "Please." When they receive it, have them say, "Thank you." As they get older, dinnertime conversation can center on "What was the highlight of your day?", "Tell me the best thing that happened today?" If they hit you with a negative comment ask them, "What did you learn from that?" Or "What's the silver lining in that situation?" These questions get the parent out of the habit of asking "How was school today?" and the child from answering with a bunch of complaints. If the child is struggling to find a positive response, offer him or her a little help, but don't let them off the hook too easily. You are, after all, supporting your child in becoming a healthier, happier adult.

Ali reveals, "Gratitude has helped me be a better parent. It's helped me appreciate my children, their insight, and unique toddler perspective on the world as they see it. I find that I listen more intently to my children. And believe it or not, my three- and four-year old girls have pretty amazing things to say. By telling them I appreciate their good behavior, it acts as positive reinforcement. Plus, they have picked up on that and when I come home from work, they tell me they love me and ask me how my day was. Or they thank me at mealtime and say "Thanks Mom–you're the best cook!" While being appreciative of them, they in turn, have become appreciative of me." Ali's story demonstrates that listening to your child and asking positive questions creates a strong bond between a parent and their child.

☞ Today, take a few moments and write a letter to each of your children, letting them know the specific things that you love and why you are proud of them. Leave it on their pillow so they can read it on their own, or read it to them. You will create a meaningful treasure that they will value for a long time (even if they don't say so.)

My child's reaction to my note was:

_____

_____

_____

_____

_____

_____

_____

_____

_____

_____

_____

_____

_____

_____

THE UPSIDE OF DOWN TIMES

"Cheerfulness is the best promoter of health and is as friendly to the mind as to the body."
— **Joseph Addison**

Although there have been many educators in the field, Dr. Martin Seligman of the University of Pennsylvania pioneered the study of positive education. Known as the Father of Modern Positive Psychology, Dr. Seligman introduced the topic for the first time in his book *Authentic Happiness: Using the New Positive Psychology to Realize Your Potential for Lasting Fulfillment.*

In Seligman's book, *Learned Optimism*, he states, "I believe that traditional wisdom is incomplete. A composer can have all the talent of Mozart and a passionate desire to succeed, but if he believes he cannot compose music, he will come to nothing. He will not try hard enough. He will give up too soon when the elusive right melody takes too long to materialize." Dr. Seligman believes that by changing the way a person thinks, the person can change not only his or her outlook on life, but the quality of that life as well.

Seligman also studied the effects of the "gratitude intervention." He randomly assigned volunteers to various "interventions," and assessed their happiness before and after. In the gratitude intervention, people are asked to think about a person who was kind or helpful to them but has never been thanked for it. The volunteer then writes a one-page letter of thanks, makes an appointment with the target person, and reads the letter to him or her. The volunteers who are randomly assigned to do this task show significant increases in happiness six months after completing it.

OTHERS

Stanford University offers a happiness class which is quite popular. During the first week of class and again at the end, instructors survey students' stress levels to measure the effectiveness of the lessons. On average, they have found stress levels actually decreased by 27% by the end of the class. (How many college courses can make that claim?)

Course assignments include researching what leads to happiness and what doesn't. Students try out techniques on friends and family and then report their findings in class. One activity required students to seek out food service employees, janitors, groundskeepers, and other "invisible people" and thank them for what they do around campus.

One student shared with the class that he told his dorm's cleaning woman that it was nice to have a clean shower every day. He recounted that she burst into tears. She informed him that she'd been cleaning at Stanford for sixteen years, and this was the first time anyone had ever thanked her. Class members find that they receive a huge payoff in good feelings without having to expend a great deal of effort to positively impact other's lives.

Harvard University also offers a happiness class that is affecting the life of the professor as well the students'. Professor Tal Ben-Shahar began his career as an instructor of the class Positive Psychology. He is now a sought-after author, speaker, and consultant in the field. Ben-Shahar reveals, "Students are attracted to this kind of class because they feel that it's making a real difference in their lives. The quest for happiness has always been an innate human yearning, dating back to the times of Confucius and Aristotle. The difference today is that for the first time we have a science of happiness."

In this class, students study articles, essays, and research reports from a variety of scientific publications. Dr. Ben-Shahar also contributes personally to the class by having them read his book *Happier: Learn the Secrets to Daily Joy and Lasting Fulfillment.*

When the class started in 1999, twenty students attended. In 2006, the class attracted more than 850 students, making it the most popular class at Harvard—beating out the long-time title holder Introduction to Economics. (I don't know about you, but to me, that's really not surprising.)

When Elizabeth enrolled in Ben-Shahar's class, she was skeptical; after all, she wanted to take a "real" psychology class. As she progressed through the lessons, she experienced profound changes in her attitude. Before the class, she was fanatical about her grades and fixated on the future. The class helped her to take the time to live in the moment. She also learned to express her gratitude more openly with others. "A lot of people think positive psychology means walking around with a smile on your face," says Elizabeth, "It's not that. It's learning to take the good with the bad and learning to make the most of your life."

The study of gratitude continues to provoke interest in the collegiate world. In 2012, the Greater Good Science Center at the University of California, Berkeley—in collaboration with the University of California, Davis—announced a $5.9 million, three-year project on Expanding the Science and Practice of Gratitude. According to their website, the goals of this initiative are to:

- "Expand the scientific database of gratitude, particularly in the key areas of human health, personal and relational well-being, and developmental science"

- "Promote evidence-based practices of gratitude in medical, educational, and organizational settings and in schools, workplaces, homes and communities," and in so doing…

- "Engage the public in a larger cultural conversation about the role of gratitude in civil society."

We don't lack proof that happiness and appreciation deeply affect our well-being. The only thing we have to do is take this information to heart and incorporate more positivity into our own lives. The choice is up to us.

If you are interested in learning more details of the science behind the study of gratitude, check out books by authors in the field of positive psychology. A list of suggested reading can also be found in the appendix. This list is not comprehensive by any means. These are books that I personally find inspiring.

Notes:

_____

_____

_____

_____

_____

_____

_____

_____

_____

_____

_____

THE UPSIDE OF DOWN TIMES

"Gratitude unlocks the fullness of life. It turns what we have into enough and more. It turns denial into acceptance, chaos to order, confusion to clarity. It turns problems into gifts, failures into successes, the unexpected into perfect timing, and mistakes into important events ... gratitude makes sense of our past, brings peace for today, and creates a vision for tomorrow."
– Melodie Beattie

Sometimes we find it tricky to be thankful because we focus too much on comparing ourselves to others. We cause undue stress by crafting the wrong type of connection. For example, when we weigh ourselves against others who possess more than we do, we may feel inferior. If you must measure yourself up to someone who is more successful, do it in a way that inspires you to use your talents to catapult yourself to his or her level.

You might also compare yourself against people who have considerably less than you. On one hand, this could enable you to see how blessed you are. On the other hand, it might cause you to look down on those less fortunate. If the latter is the case, here are two words for you: STOP IT!

There is a classic skit on "Mad TV" with Bob Newhart that effectively illustrates this point. (If you haven't seen it, it's worth watching on YouTube.) Newhart plays the role of a psychiatrist who can cure any patient with two words: STOP IT! No matter the excuse his patient provides for his/her current emotional state, his response is "STOP IT!" I now regularly use "STOP IT" on myself. It makes me laugh because of the skit, and I realize that I have the power to end any negative stream of thought I choose.

OTHERS

Before my discovering of the power of "STOP IT," I experienced some defining moments which unlocked the fullness of my life. The following story taught me how the power of gratitude could turn what I had into enough.

A few months before my 30th birthday, I was overtaken by a deep depression. I compared my life to the lives of my friends—and not in a very favorable way. My friends were all married; they lived in beautiful homes, drove nice cars, and had adorable kids. What did I have? I was divorced from my first husband and was currently dating Mr. Right-Now. I rented a house, leased a car, and lived with my four cats—a recipe for dating disaster. I was in one heck of a temper and I couldn't shake my bleak mood.

Finally, I reached my saturation point. I started asking myself questions: Wasn't I supposed to be a positive thinker? What about all the books and seminars attended over the past seven years? Did all that positive education mean nothing? Who was I to allow myself to drown in this pool of negativity? Big changes needed to happen—quickly.

Grudgingly, I probed further: "Well, what DO I have to be grateful for?" The unexpected answer emerged over a period of time. After all, the very things that I envied my friends for having were, in effect, all the things I didn't want at this point in my life anyway.

I thought, "Wait a minute! I'm 29 years old and feel great. There's no house to maintain, no husband to take care of, no car to depreciate, and no kids to fuss over. I can do what I want, when I want, with whomever I please. I'm not tied down to my location. There's no one to answer to other than myself. Wow! These are the BEST times of my life!" That simple reframing revolutionized everything. My mood started to shift.

THE UPSIDE OF DOWN TIMES

I broke up with Mr. Right-Now, a man whom I had been dating for nine months. I wanted to clear a space in my life for Mr. Right, whoever he was.

Soon after my 'gratitude adjustment,' it happened. I went to the gym to teach my weekly aerobics class. Glancing across the room, I saw a guy that gave me a physical reaction like I had never experienced before. Whoosh! It literally felt like fireworks were shooting out of the top of my head. (Holy cow, what was THAT?!!!) Several of my friends were waiting at the back of the room for my class to begin and I informed them that I had "just seen the most beautiful man I had ever seen in my life." They replied, "Oh, Lisa, you say that all the time." And I said, "Oh no, you don't understand."

As fate would have it, a few weeks later, while this man waited for an exercise bike, I casually sidled over to him and inquired, "So, have you been working out here long?" His name was Scott, and we spoke for about twenty minutes. Not wanting him to think I was a stalker, I nonchalantly let him know that it was nice to meet him and I would catch up with him later. I proceeded to go to the lat machine and put on as much weight as I could muster. I brought the weights down really slowly, so that if Scott was watching, he could check out my awesome back muscles. To my delight, he was paying attention and soon afterwards, he asked me out to lunch.

That morning, I told my colleague about him: "I'm having lunch with this really cute guy from the gym, but I don't think it was going to go anywhere." She asked me why, and I responded, "Because he's 32, he lives at home, and he's poor." But when Scott walked in through the door, those sentiments disappeared. I still remember exactly what he was wearing: dark blue double-breasted blazer, khaki pants, and a great tie. Stick a fork in me – I was done.

OTHERS

Seven months after our first date, we were engaged. We married a year and a half later. At this moment, we've been together for 18 years and I still feel like a honeymooner. Scott is the biggest blessing in my life. He supports me in my entrepreneurial adventures and is truly behind me, cheering all the way. I am extremely grateful for him.

Considering all the stars that had to align in order for me to meet Scott, it came to me that everything happened because of gratitude. I assessed my blessings instead of concentrating on lack. Most importantly, I took the requisite actions to meet Scott. Sure, it was risky "sidling up" to a good-looking stranger at the gym, but I did — and it's paid off handsomely (pun intended).

☞ Set a timer at various intervals throughout the day to "check in" with your thoughts. At those moments, stop what you're doing and observe your thinking patterns. If you find yourself dwelling in a state of negativity-STOP IT! Figure out a way to change your current opinion to one that is more positive and make this process your ongoing happy habit.

Noticing my thought patterns throughout the day, I discovered:

_____

_____

_____

_____

_____

_____

_____

_____

_____

THE UPSIDE OF DOWN TIMES

"Gratitude is to marriage as oil is to an engine. It needs to be applied liberally and throughout and is of such importance, that a fresh supply must be added regularly to ensure success and longevity."
— **Matthew Smith**

How does gratitude strengthen a marriage? The marital relationship can be the most significant bond we have with any other human being. Research by Dr. John Gottman of the Gottman Relationship Institute discovered that happily married couples retain at least a 5:1 ratio of positive to negative interactions. For every negative dealing, disagreement, or hurt feeling, the offending spouse should offer five positive, loving, caring, or playful interactions to counterbalance it.

Relationships thrive when we bring more positive energy than negative energy into them. However, what about our negative communications? How do these exchanges, no matter how small, affect our connections in the long run?

These questions bring to mind a story I heard about Little Johnny. Little Johnny was a bully. He had no friends due to his meanness and hassling of others all the time. His mother, growing weary of her son's behavior, decided to teach him a lesson. She brought out a bucket of nails and told Little Johnny that every time he disrespected someone else, he must take a nail and pound it into the picket fence in the backyard.

Over the next couple weeks, Little Johnny did just that, furiously pounding nails for each of his infractions. As he became more aware of his actions to others, his behavior began to change. He wasn't mean anymore.

Little Johnny's mom had observed this transformation and she now suggested that every time he was nice to someone, he could remove one of the nails. Sure enough, over the course of several weeks, Johnny plucked out the nails until they were all gone.

What was left? Holes.

Negative comments uttered to our spouse, our children, or anyone else for that matter can significantly hurt them and cause a hole in the relationship that may never be filled. We need to carefully consider our remarks at all times. Just like Mom used to say, "If you can't say anything nice, don't say anything at all." Better to be patient and kind than to potentially destroy a loving relationship with a spur-of-the-moment, callous criticism.

Ali and her husband have experienced the benefits of gratitude in their marriage. She says, "While my husband and I have always had a great relationship with communication and the ability to tell each other what we're thinking without consequence, which gets interesting when he says, 'Oh, you're wearing that huh?' and I say, 'Yep.' We tell each other how much we appreciate each other and why. When I tell him I appreciate him, I don't just say 'thanks' or 'I appreciate you,' but I say, 'Wow, thank you for being a stay-at-home dad. Our kids are lucky to have you at home and spend time with you. Not every guy would be up for that.' Then he feels appreciated, and he feels really special because he knows a lot of other guys who wouldn't do what he does. Specific appreciation goes a long way."

If you want to make an immediate impact in your marriage, support your spouse out loud. Notice the little things he or she accomplishes around the house or the caring gestures made during the day. Small considerations can create a big difference. When you first acknowledge your partner for the thoughtful things that he or she performs all the time—taking out the trash, emptying the dishwasher, picking up after the kids—he or she may suspiciously think, "Ok, what do you really want?" However, if you turn it into a habit, chances are that you're going to receive those same positive comments in return.

Jess Alberts and Angela Trethewey have researched how people in successful relationships deal with division of household chores. They discovered that splitting tasks doesn't generally become an issue if one partner expresses approval for the contributions of the others.

When one spouse deems the labor split unfair, that individual tends to experience dissatisfaction with the marriage and more likely to believe he or she would be better off divorced. It all comes down to gratefulness. If you feel that your partner appreciates your efforts, especially if you perform the majority of the tasks at hand, you feel more inclined to cultivate a greater sense of fairness, satisfaction, and gratitude in the relationship.

The best wedding advice I have ever received originated from my friend Robbie. She said, "Never do something at the beginning of a marriage that you don't want to be doing twenty years from now." That guidance has served me well. For example, we established early in our relationship that Scott would mow the <u>lawn</u> and I would do the <u>laundry</u>. Thankfully, I have never had to use the lawnmower. (I did attempt to use the snow blower on a single occasion, but that unmitigated disaster will never be repeated.) He derives the benefits of being outside as well as having freshly laundered clothing folded neatly for him, and I don't have to worry about outdoor manual labor. It works for us.

The next time your partner calls during the day just to say, "I love you," see it as a gift and not an inconvenient intrusion in your busy day. When you come home from a long day at work and dinner is sitting on the table, take an extra moment for a lingering kiss and a heartfelt "I appreciate you." Make thankfulness for your loved one a part of your everyday dialogue.

If you're not already recognizing your significant other, make a commitment to start today. Even if you've been married "forever," you may find it helps you feel like you're dating again.

You may think, "Well, he/she had better start being nicer to me before I start appreciating him/her." Do yourself a favor and get over your big, bad self! (STOP IT!) If you truly desire to enrich your relationship, you have the power to do so.

If you're out of practice, your big question may be: "How do I begin?" First, take some time to make a list of all the things your spouse does for you, even if he or she's been performing it for years. Make the list as long as you can and reflect on what it feels like to have those things done for you.

Think back to the beginning of your relationship. Remember how every little thing your spouse did gave you butterflies? What attracted you to your special person?

Remind yourself of all the reasons that you wanted to spend every minute of the day with him or her. Recall the first time you saw "the one." Your first date. Your first kiss. The joy you felt each time he or she came over to pick you up. Savor those moments and imagine what it would be like to treat your mate the same way you did back then. If all else fails, "fake it 'til you make it".

☞ A simple exercise entails recalling a moment when you were as happy as you have ever been with your partner—your wedding day, a special vacation, or your experience as first-time parents. Fully experience the emotions you felt on that occasion; immerse wholly in your imagination. Now, picture how you're going to feel when your partner comes home tonight. How will you greet him or her; what will you do to show you care? Visualize the smile and the warm hug you'll receive. Enjoy the sensation. Feel good? Now you're ready to proceed.

Start the conversation with "I haven't really taken the time to let you know how much I appreciate you, and I want to do a better job at expressing how grateful I am for you." Then take a few minutes to explain in detail some of the things your husband/wife does that you value. Expect nothing in return. Just let your partner absorb the feeling of acknowledgement. Continue to share on a regular basis—sooner or later, your spouse will realize it's the "new you."

From time to time, write your mate a love letter or quick note. When I come into my office and find a message that says "I love you" from my husband, I can guarantee you that that note does NOT get thrown away. When you tell your spouse how much you appreciate him or her, you create a memory. When you write it down in a note, card, or letter, you create a treasure.

At my Grategy® workshops, an exercise that the participants complete includes composing a letter to "someone who needs to hear from them." One of the attendees chose to address a thank-you note to her husband. When we bumped into each other a few days later, she shared that she had left the memo on the counter, and when her husband came home from work, he saw it and asked, "What's this?" She answered, "It's something that I wrote to you." He read it, and then, very carefully, folded the note and put it in his wallet. That's a treasure. Now he has wonderful, visible proof of his wife's love for him. Isn't it time you gave someone you love a treasure? As leadership expert John Maxwell says, "What you appreciate, appreciates." Makes sense, doesn't it?

☞ Make a commitment to write a note of appreciation to someone at least once a month. Once you experience how good it feels to do so, challenge yourself to do it once a week. Create your own treasure in the form of the written word and make someone's day special.

I commit to writing a note today to:

_____

_____

_____

_____

_____

_____

_____

_____

_____

_____

_____

_____

_____

THE UPSIDE OF DOWN TIMES

"Remember, my sentimental friend, that a heart is not judged by how much you love, but by how much you are loved by others."
— **The Wizard of Oz**

Although the bond that we create with our significant other is one of the strongest connections we have, it's important to "make new friends and keep the old" (former Girl Scouts may remember this little ditty). We have no idea how the people in our lives or those we meet along our journey will open doors that we would have never otherwise imagined. "One is silver and the other gold," ends the Girl Scouts' song, with the former representing new friends and the latter symbolizing the old.

When my position was eliminated, I joined the ranks of people who lost their jobs due to downsizing, right-sizing, lay-offs, off-shoring, restructuring, etc. Although I maintained a good attitude most of the time, I have to admit, there were plenty of moments when I was scared. I made good money in sales and my income wasn't easy to replace.

Contemplating my situation, I knew I had many choices. I could find another sales job, go back to school or change careers. I could choose the road of many before me and wallow in self-pity and despair. Instead, I decided to put myself out there, networking like a madwoman and figuring that from those meetings, mutual benefits would occur through developing relationships.

Strengthening the bonds with my friends and associates by spending more quality time became important to me as well. I was open to the upside of the hand that fate had dealt, and ready to receive the good that life was about to offer—with no idea what it was going to look like.

The down times weren't to last long. Just a few weeks after my termination, the first of many interesting opportunities presented itself. My friend, Cindy, introduced me to her friend from college, Sheri, who owned a training company. We met for coffee, and she offered me the opportunity to conduct presentation skills training classes on a contract basis. The class structure was great and I started teaching a few classes a month. It felt good to do something I loved (and get paid for it). What a concept! Life started to pick up speed and I was enjoying the ride.

Through a series of "coincidences," I was invited to be in not one, but two, self-development films. I was featured alongside some of the biggest names in the speaking industry, working with people whose material I had been studying for years. The "Keeper of the Keys" premiered on the red carpet in Las Vegas. "The Gratitude Experiment" followed soon after.

The publication of my first book, *With Excellence*, helped me achieve my dream of being an author. In addition to these exciting moments, I was offered a number of fabulous speaking gigs as well. I give thanks for each of these chances and guess what? More of them keep appearing in my life.

Noted director and screenwriter Woody Allen once stated, "Eighty percent of success is just showing up," and I wholeheartedly agree. The preceding breaks presented themselves because I put myself in situations to meet the right people, or at least the individuals who knew that the right people were the key (pun intended).

THE UPSIDE OF DOWN TIMES

In the beginning of my speaking career, I spoke quite often for free. Maybe "free" isn't the right word—I spoke in exchange for food, for wine, for trinkets. I even once spoke in return for catnip. Yes, catnip, and here's how it happened: I was presenting my talk for the second year in a row at a local high school for a group called the "Glass Ceiling Girls." The instructor remembered from the previous year's program that I had cats. As part of my reward, she included a live catnip plant for my cats to enjoy (they did.) You see, when you do a good job, people remember you. And, when they remember details about you, it makes an impression. Will I speak to this group again next year? Absolutely. Why? The instructor made me feel special.

No matter where you are in your career (or lack thereof), being grateful for all the advantages in your life will help. You have housing, transportation, clothes. You have family and friends who love and support you. Open yourself to possibilities in your relationships. Don't discount any prospect—give it a chance, for it may pleasantly surprise you.

Revel in whatever you have in your life. Your energy will shift and doors will start to open for you that will exceed your expectations. Bask in the knowledge that you are making progress, even if it doesn't always seem like anything is happening. Your relationships are not only there for mutual affection and encouragement; they help you venture further than you ever thought possible.

☞ Right now, take a deep breath and visualize five blessings in your life. Experience the full emotion of your good fortune until you find yourself smiling. Use this exercise several times a day. It only takes a minute, and the effects will "positively" help you through your day.

OTHERS

Five blessings in my life are:

_____

_____

_____

_____

_____

_____

_____

_____

_____

_____

_____

_____

_____

_____

_____

_____

_____

_____

_____

_____

_____

_____

_____

_____

_____

_____

_____

_____

Chapter 4

Wealth

Thank and Grow Rich

"Try measuring your wealth by what you are rather than by what you have. Put the tape measure around your heart rather than around your bank account."
– Anonymous

In this last section, we'll look at the role appreciation plays in the accumulation of wealth in personal and professional success. (Honestly, by show of hands, how many of you turned to this chapter first? Just checking.)

Let's face it, no matter how much money we have, chances are, we could always use more. After all, it can make life easier, even more fun. We can use money to purchase the latest gadgets, a fabulous new car, or a house on the beach. At the very least, it puts food on the table, pays the rent, and keeps the utility company from turning off the heat.

It's been written that, "The love of money is the root of all evil", but, if looked at positively, money can supply mosquito nets and fresh water to third world countries, provide shelter for the homeless and food for the hungry.

Money is neither good nor evil, it just is.

WEALTH

Wealth can come in many forms. It could be a comforting hand, a priceless friendship, or a patient teacher. It could be the paycheck you receive at the end of a busy work week, or the gratitude and appreciation which you incorporate into your life.

Whether we would like to admit it or not, our current financial situation could very well be a direct result of our attitude of gratitude. It's a known fact that people who pursue money at the expense of their integrity, their relationships and their health tend to take the goodness in their lives for granted.

There are times when life gets in my way. I get overwhelmed as I'm struggling to fit way too much into my day and my gratitude practice falls to the wayside. I feel the difference in my mood, in my relationships and in my finances when that happens. I have to remind myself to get back to my gratitude practice. When I start up again, there is an immediate difference in my attitude - my stress level decreases and my ability to find joy and have fun again increases.

I have noticed that when I am grateful for what I have - when I am pursuing my passion, and enjoying my life - I receive the finances I need, exactly when I require them. On the other hand, when I am stressing out, trying to force circumstances to occur, and attempting to figure out where the next paycheck is coming from, the money stops: money seems to sense my fear and in those times I scare money away. When I release my anxiety and trust that I am on the right path, I attract money. It happens.

Being thankful, giving appreciation to others and receiving wealth in a variety of forms can increase our bottom line, because gratefulness helps us attract more of what we want in life and less of what we don't

THE UPSIDE OF DOWN TIMES

Unfortunately, we live in a time of immediate gratification. When we want something, we want it NOW. We work hard and we feel entitled to getting the biggest and best of everything that is available to us. However, when we take the time to be grateful for the things we already have, we attract more of them.

Want more abundance? Look for it. When you are counting your pennies, nickels and dollars, make sure you are counting your blessings as well.

☞ What would you like to attract more of in your life right now? What do you already have in that area for which you can be grateful?

_____

_____

_____

_____

_____

_____

_____

_____

_____

_____

_____

_____

_____

_____

_____

_____

_____

_____

_____

WEALTH

"To receive more, we must be willing to give more...It is expressly at those times when we feel needy that we will benefit the most from giving."
– **Ruth Ross**

Renee is a sales rep who decided to put the power of gratitude to work with her clients. She says, "I put my selfishness aside and started to approach customers with gratitude and treated them like they were an important guest in my home. Wow, what an impact it made on my sales! I shot up to 400% increase in up-selling and cross-selling the customer. I went from being at the bottom of the group to the top seller of the group instantly. My supervisor could not believe it. She asked what my secret was. I told her that I changed my approach to the customer.

"I just started thinking about their satisfaction and continually let them know how much we appreciated them calling in and then gave the offer. Then, I had customer after customer saying they would return next week for additional weekly specials. After the sale was complete, I would take a few seconds and let my heart well up with thankfulness and really appreciate that the customer was open and responsive before I moved on to the next customer. Then, at the end of the day, I would meditate and contemplate with a heart full of appreciation and thankfulness."

Renee not only showed her clientele gratitude externally, she did the inner work that made her results more profound. She allowed herself to "well up with thankfulness" and she visualized her success. By seeing it happen in advance, she helped to make it a reality.

Sam also does the inner work on her business. She started keeping a gratitude journal and soon thereafter, she saw a 25% increase in her insurance business during a time when her company was losing seventeen agents in her area, all of whom claimed that they could not acquire any new customers. Sam, however, was unwilling to participate in their dismay, and her business continues to thrive.

One way Sam thanks her customers is by telling them how much she appreciates them on a regular basis. She hired a part-time person to call all of her clients every year and express the agency's gratitude for their business. On the road to customer satisfaction, there may be little traffic on the extra mile, but Sam is in a lane of her own.

An Accenture 2007 Global Customer Satisfaction Survey found that nearly 60% of respondents claim that customer service is the main reason they do business with a company, beating out price (55%), product (34%), and convenience (34%). Companies with a reputation for delivering shoddy service will experience a steep challenge ahead when it comes to growth.

Bottom line? Don't take your clients for granted—ever. In his book *Swim with the Sharks Without Being Eaten Alive*, Harvey Mackay introduces the Mackay 66 Profile. Over the course of their client relationships, Mackay and his staff strive to answer sixty-six questions about each customer (Not all at once, of course!). By the time they're done, they know practically everything they will ever need to know about that buyer. Mackay has built a successful envelope empire based on getting to know his clientele.

Along that line, Emily, a financial planner, uses a variety of approaches to show appreciation to her clients, from sending flowers to making charitable donations in their names. She looks for unique ways to let her regulars know she cares about them. She also hosts an annual client appreciation event because she believes "there is nothing like a party to say thanks!" Emily shares, "As I understand it, the more I give, the more I receive. I don't worry about financials from day to day. When I find I'm becoming selfish, life gets pretty ugly. For me, the concept of giving just works."

If you work for a company or have your own business, how can you incorporate a 'grategy®' - gratitude strategy - to let your customers know that you value them?

 Here are some ideas to get started:

1. **Follow up regularly**. In most cases, there should not be a 90 day period of time in which your customers do not hear from you. Exceed your customer's expectations and you will receive opportunities for repeat business.

2. **Resolve complaints quickly**. Take care of your customer's questions and problems right away. It's often not the superior service we provide when things are going well that get noticed, it's how we handle the problems.

3. **Increase your value**. Become a valued resource for your customers. Building long term relationships with people you know, like and trust will get your further than a one shot business deal. Zig Ziglar once said, "You can get anything you want in life if you help enough other people get what they want."

THE UPSIDE OF DOWN TIMES

☞ How can you incorporate your own gratitude strategy into your business? Write down as many ways as you can think of to "touch" your customers.

_____

_____

_____

_____

_____

_____

_____

_____

_____

_____

_____

_____

_____

_____

_____

_____

_____

_____

_____

_____

_____

_____

_____

_____

_____

WEALTH

"You simply will not be the same person two months from now after consciously giving thanks each day for the abundance that exists in your life. And, you will have set in motion an ancient spiritual law: the more you have and are grateful for, the more will be given you."
— **Sarah Ban Breathnach**

"Samantha" has worked for many years for a research company which has gone through several ownership changes (and none of them have been good). Under constant pressure to perform, she sometimes labors late into the night and through the weekends. Because she works from home, her employer expects her to get her work done, no matter the effect on her personal life. She suffers from the physical manifestations of stress: migraines, joint pains, and weight problems. Although she knows she needs to find an alternative, she continues to complain without taking action to move forward. She feels stuck.

I asked Samantha to imagine losing her job. At first, she breathed a sigh of relief, and I could see her physically relax. Then reality set in, and she realized what would happen to her family without that additional income. How would they pay for their son's college, their family vacations, and the "toys" that they both enjoy? Would they eat out as much or be forced to cut down on their social events? Once she visualized the negative impact, she felt a little more grateful for its existence. It wasn't much, but it was a start.

How can you be thankful for a job you dislike immensely? Start where you are. Consider that if you work eight hours a day, you must enjoy some aspect of it. Maybe it's an activity that only takes up a minuscule part of your day, but it's satisfying. Begin there and be grateful.

THE UPSIDE OF DOWN TIMES

If you don't get along with a boss or coworker, for the next two months, write down one or two things that you like about him/her. No need to tell the individual in question about this practice or change anything you're doing. Just spend a few moments imagining something genuinely good about your situation. YOU will change, and over time, others will notice. Your new attitude could lead to an improved relationship with that person, or a promotion, or a transfer to another department. Take the necessary steps towards transforming your outlook and your circumstances will positively change.

If you are stuck In a job that you dislike, ask yourself the question, "What would happen if I didn't have this job?" Could you pay your bills, take care of your family, and use your talents? You may discover that you'd be just fine, and the knowledge gives you the impetus to leave. Maybe you'll find that you're grateful about certain aspects of the job and that it's not so horrible after all. Asking the question is your first step.

No matter how you feel about your current place of employment, write down all of the things for which you are grateful on the job. Do you receive free training? Do you have nice co-workers? Does the company offer a flexible schedule? Do you have decent insurance? Is the income at least 'better than unemployment?' You may be surprised by the length of your list.

Things I like about my job:

_____

_____

_____

_____

WEALTH

_____

_____

_____

_____

_____

_____

_____

_____

_____

_____

_____

_____

_____

_____

_____

_____

_____

_____

_____

_____

_____

_____

_____

With so many people focusing on these down times, getting stuck in the muck of their own negativity, those who are willing to concentrate on the upside and consider all the things that are going well will fare much better in the long run. Positive people set themselves apart by being unique. They bring a smile instead of a complaint. They don't try to fit in, they stand out.

Bonus Section

How Can Gratitude Bring Wealth to Your Business?

"Make it a habit to tell people thank you. To express your appreciation, sincerely and without the expectation of anything in return. Truly appreciate those around you, and you'll soon find many others around you. Truly appreciate life, and you'll find that you have more of it."
— **Ralph Marston**

My company, Grategy®, was founded based on a study conducted by noted speaker, author and copywriter, Dan Kennedy. The study shows that when a customer stops doing business with a company, sixty-eight percent of the time, it's because that consumer feels "ignored, unappreciated or taken for granted." When we take the time to show gratitude to our patrons, we develop a base of loyal customers as well as raving fans.

Michelle attributes the growing success of her home-based business to sending cards to her clients. Not only do they receive a thank-you card after placing an order, she mails cards for no reason other than to say, "Thank you, and I love you as a customer." She elaborates, "I try to make it very clear to my customers how much I appreciate them and how much they're helping me towards a specific goal. They're the most important people to me and so I let them know."

Michelle knows that she holds the power to choose her attitude. "You can choose to have a good day every day or you can choose to have a bad day. And I always made the decision that no matter what's going on in my life, no one would ever know what was going bad in my life."

Because of her thank-you notes, Michelle receives tons of referrals. She also keeps a file of all the happy e-mails and messages from satisfied customers. "We all have bad days, and it's nice to be able to go back to that file. It makes me feel like I have a friend or two out there somewhere." In her e-mails she includes the quote: "Be kinder than you think is necessary because everyone's fighting their own battles." And she truly believes that. "There is no other way to be," she explains.

On several occasions during my sales career I have quipped, "You can keep the money, just give me the plaque!" It wasn't a serious comment, of course, because that would be just crazy, but it felt good to be on stage, congratulated by management and recognized by my peers. It was a reward in itself. I lived for those moments and while I needed my paycheck, I needed something else too; to be acknowledged and appreciated.

In the course of my Grategy® training programs, I've heard comments from several employers, "Why should I thank my employees for doing their job? After all, that's what they're being paid to do. Their paycheck is their thanks." These complainers are generally the same bosses who gripe when their staff does not put any additional effort toward their job. When you treat your personnel with thoughtful consideration, they in turn put forth more effort, are easier to work with, and get along better with others. Expressing appreciation to your workers for a job well done is an important way to increase professional satisfaction and employee retention.

THE UPSIDE OF DOWN TIMES

A study by the University of Florida found that people don't necessarily leave their job, they leave their boss. Researchers discovered that a stimulating work setting was more significant than the pay grade. Unhappy employees are less likely to give any extra effort to get their jobs done. Happy employees, on the other hand, take on additional tasks, work longer hours or occasional weekends, and generally feel more content at work. Who would you rather have working for, or with you?

While in the welding industry, I occasionally received my commission statement with a handwritten note from Bud, the corporate big Kahuna. Usually it comprised just a few words: "Great job, Lisa!" or "Awesome month." Those words meant the world to me. Even though it was a long time ago, I still treasure those notes because someone acknowledged the good job I was doing and it made me work harder for the company. Bud was a rare man in corporate America, and his personal correspondence was very special. When Bud retired, the company lost a huge part of what made it special. We need more Buds in the world—will you be one?

If you haven't appreciated someone who works with you, make it a point to do so today. Sometimes, if it's not a common occurrence, the recipient of your comments may look for an ulterior motive. You can say something like, "I know I haven't taken the time lately to let you know how much I appreciate you, and I'm sorry about that. I am grateful for you and the excellent work you do around here. Thank you."

According to an article in Fortune magazine, John Kralik, author of *A Simple Act of Gratitude*, started writing thank-you notes in 2008 as his life and law firm were both suffering. His goal: Write one appreciative message per day for a year. Kralik soon saw a definite link between his appreciation notes and his business thriving again. He reveals, "As you take care of the paying clients, they pay even faster. They value you. ... When you're feeling especially crummy, it's a good time to sit down and write about 10 thank-you notes."

Laura owns an IT consulting company and similarly has seen the power of positive reception in her business growth. She sends a handwritten thank-you message to every new client and goes out of her way to support him or her, even if the tasks are not connected to paying work. She asks in-depth questions to explore how to serve them better. For an added personal touch, she includes a line in her invoices that states, "I appreciate your business." Due in part to her exceptional service and follow-up, Laura's company has recently been recognized as one of the top ten small businesses in her region.

When you read these stories you probably think, "Isn't this just common sense?" There's absolutely nothing "common" about common sense. Gratitude works so well in today's business environment because...(drum roll, please)...very few people do it (or do it well)! With deadlines to meet, quotas to achieve, and sales management on our backs, we focus so intently on pounding the pavement for new "blood" that we neglect the shoppers we've worked hard to bring on board.

Acknowledge people. Make a heartfelt connection with everyone you meet and you will have them all at "hello." Take care of them, treat them like a valued part of your business and your life, and enhance their business experience with you and you will keep them from saying "goodbye."

☞ How can you implement the ideas from this chapter today? Simply pick one of your favorite customers—not necessarily the most profitable one, but someone you enjoy working with. Think about something you can do to bring a smile to his or her face. Flowers? Home-made goodies? A customized limerick? Do something nice with no expectation of return. Both you and your client will feel good, and you'll once again distinguish yourself in his or her eyes.

It's been said that we spend the first half of our life using our health to achieve wealth. Then we spend the second half of our life using our wealth to realize health. Let's do what we can while we have our health AND get to where we want to be with our finances as well.

☞ Creative ways I can bring a smile to my customers:

_____

_____

_____

_____

_____

_____

_____

_____

_____

_____

_____

_____

_____

_____

A New Beginning: Choosing Gratitude

"As we express our gratitude, we must never forget that the highest appreciation is not to utter words, but to live by them."
— **John F. Kennedy**

In this book, we've explored the amazing power of gratitude; from its effects on our Self, Health, relationships with Others, and our Wealth. We have also touched on how a grateful mindset has the power to improve your business and your bottom line.

In order that you don't get overwhelmed trying to change everything at once, pick one of these four areas of S.H.O.W. and simply focus on improving your life one section at a time.

During our journey, we have explored the benefits of gratitude on the **self,** and found that by keeping a gratitude journal, we can help change our perspective on what happens in our lives.

We studied the influence of an attitude of gratitude on our **health,** and found direct consequences, i.e.; when we feel aggravated, it affects the performance of our heart, and when we are angry, we deplete our immune system.

We understand we should incorporate appreciation into our relationships with **others,** because those are the ones who can so easily be taken for granted.

THE UPSIDE OF DOWN TIMES

We learned that what we focus our attention on expands, including our **wealth**. If we concentrate on financial lack, we will attract it, and to create abundance we must look for it.

Taking the time to show gratitude in every area of our lives, can indeed help us find the upside in down times.

Everything in life happens for a reason and although we don't always know what that purpose is, sooner or later it makes sense to us. Whether it is the loss of a job, the end of a relationship, the illness of a loved one or any other event we would not have chosen, our perspective makes a huge difference in how we handle what's been put on our plate.

When you perceive things as going "wrong" in your life, stop for a moment and take the time to appreciate all the good you have so that you will attract more of what you want.

Our lives consist of many choices. We can choose to drown in our despair or we can look for the highlights. Here's a story that sums up a an attitude of gratitude versus ingratitude:

Twin brothers were celebrating their birthday. One of the boys was a negativist and the other was an optimist. When the negative boy opened his presents, he grumbled and complained about each gift, nothing was good enough or it wasn't exactly what he was looking for. The parents were used to their sons' polar-opposite reactions and so they thought they would try something different with the optimist son, to see what happened.

The optimistic little boy was shown to a room piled high with manure. Rather than crying or trying to run away, he dove right in, digging through the muck with his bare hands, poop flying in all directions! His parents were baffled-what in the world is he thinking?! They ran into the room and asked the child "What ARE you doing???" Grinning, the boy responded: "With all this manure, there's just got to be a pony here somewhere!"

Things will not always go the way we want them to, and when they don't, we have two choices, we can grumble and complain, or we can look for the pony.

Remember, when we have a positive, grateful mindset, we empower ourselves to attract the very best life has to offer. So which will you choose? I hope you choose gratitude. And just in case no one has told you today – I appreciate YOU!

As you go forth, remember these words:

Be Thankful

Be thankful that you don't already have everything you desire,
If you did, what would there be to look forward to?

Be thankful when you don't know something
For it gives you the opportunity to learn.

Be thankful for the difficult times.
During those times you grow.

Be thankful for your limitations
Because they give you opportunities for improvement.

THE UPSIDE OF DOWN TIMES

Be thankful for each new challenge
Because it will build your strength and character.

Be thankful for your mistakes
They will teach you valuable lessons.

Be thankful when you're tired and weary
Because it means you've made a difference.

It is easy to be thankful for the good things.
A life of rich fulfillment comes to those who are
also thankful for the setbacks.

GRATITUDE can turn a negative into a positive.
Find a way to be thankful for your troubles
and they can become your blessings.

Author Unknown

Recommended Reading:

Attitude is Everything by Keith Harrell
Authentic Happiness by Martin E. Seligman, PhD
Chicken Soup for the Soul by Jack Canfield, Mark Victor Hansen
Count Your Blessings by Dr. John Demartini
Excuse Me Your Life Is Waiting by Lynn Grabhorn
First, Break All the Rules by Marcus Buckingham
Flow: The Psychology of Optimal Experience by Mihaly Csikszentmihalyi
From Chaos to Coherence by Doc Childre
Gratitude: Affirming the Good Things in Life by Melody Beattie
Happier by Tal Ben-Shahar
Happy For No Reason by Marci Shimoff
HeartMath Solution by Doc Childre
How Full is Your Bucket? By Tom Rath and Donald Clifton
How to Win Friends and Influence People by Dale Carnegie
Infinite Possibilities by Mike Dooley
Learned Optimism by Martin E. Seligman, PhD
Man's Search for Meaning by Viktor Frankl
Men are from Mars / Women are from Venus by John Gray, Ph.D
Psycho Cybernetics by Maxwell Maltz, MD
Success Through a Positive Mental Attitude by W. Clement Stone
Swim With the Sharks Without Being Eaten Alive by Harvey Mackay
Thanks! by Robert A. Emmons, PhD
The Four Agreements by Don Miguel Ruiz
The Hidden Messages in Water by Masaru Emoto
The How of Happiness by Sonja Lyubomirsky, Ph.D
The Power of Positive Thinking by Norman Vincent Peale
The Psychology of Gratitude by Robert A. Emmons, PhD
The Referral of a Lifetime by Tim Templeton
The Simple Abundance Companion by Sarah Ban Brethnach
The Upside of Down Times by Lisa Ryan
Think & Grow Rich by Napoleon Hill
Unlimited Power by Anthony Robbins
You Were Born Rich by Bob Proctor

Bibliography:

Alberts, Jess; Threthewey, Angela. (2007, Summer). Love, Honor, and Thank. Retrieved from http://greatergood.berkeley.edu/article/item/love_honor_thank/

Bay, Barry. (n.d.). Who's afraid of the big bad boss? Plenty of us, new FSU study shows. Retrieved from http://www.fsu.edu/news/2006/12/04/bad.boss/

Ben-Shahar, PhD, Tal. Happier. New York: McGraw-Hill, 2007

Borenstein, Seth. (2011, November 24). Giving thanks helps your psychological outlook. Retrieved from http://www.stamfordadvocate.com/news/article/Giving-thanks-helps-your-psychological-outlook-2282595.php

Caruthers, A.D. (2009, June 2). Martin Seligman: The Father of Positive Psychology. Retrieved from http://voices.yahoo.com/martin-seligman-father-positive-psychology-3376382.html?cat=5

Chapman, Gary. (2010). The 5 Love Languages: The Secret to Love That Lasts. Northfield Press.

Corporation for National and Community Service. (2007) The Health Benefits of Volunteering, A review of recent research. Retrieved from http://www.nationalservice.gov/pdf/07_0506_hbr.pdf

Demartini, Dr. John F. Count Your Blessings: The Healing Power of Gratitude and Love. Rockport, MA: Element Books, Inc., 1997

Emmons, Robert A. Thanks! How Practicing Gratitude Can Make You Happier. New York: Houghton Miffin Company, 2007

Froh, Jeffrey J. (2007, May). Gratitude in Children and Adolescents:

BIBLIOGRAPHY:

Development, Assessment, and School-Based Intervention. Retrieved from http://www.nasponline.org/publications/spf/issue2_1/froh.pdf

Froh, Jeffrey J. (2007, Summer). A Lesson in Thanks. Retrieved from http://people.hofstra.edu/Jeffrey_J_Froh/Greater%20Good.pdf

Gerdes, M.S.W, L.C.S.W., Linda. (2010, December 5). How to Be Happy No Matter What-The Power of Gratitude. Retrieved from http://www.10-minutewellness.com/blog/?p=268

Greater Good Science Center. (2012) Request for Proposals. Retrieved from http://greatergood.berkeley.edu/expandinggratitude/rfp/

Hill, Napolean. *Think and Grow Rich.* Greenwich, CT: Fawcett Crest, 1960.

Mabe, Matt. (2008, August 20). Harvard and happiness. Retrieved from http://williammartino.com/content/harvard-and-happiness

Margolies, Ph.D., Lynn. (2011) You Should be so Lucky, Dealing with Tragedy. Psych Central. Retrieved from http://psychcentral.com/lib/2011/you-should-be-so-lucky-dealing-with-tragedy/

Marsh, Jason. (2011, November 17). Tips for Keeping a Gratitude Journal. Retrieved from http://greatergood.berkeley.edu/article/item/tips_for_keeping_a_gratitude_journal/

Price, Catherine. (2007, Summer). Four Ways to Give Thanks. Retrieved from http://greatergood.berkeley.edu/article/item/four_ways_to_give_thanks/

Reijonen, Ph.D., Jori. (n.d.) Keeping a Gratitude Journal. Neuromuscular Diseases website. http://www.bellaonline.org/articles/art171318.asp retrieved 12-11-11.

Roethel, Kathryn. (2011, November 29). Stanford happiness class proves popular, helpful. Retrieved from http://www.sfgate.com/cgi-bin/article.cgi?f=/c/a/2011/11/28/BA821M2BVL.DTL#ixzz1fFVAvSqG

Ruben, Gretchen. *The Happiness Project.* New York: Harper Collins Publishers, 2009.

Ryan, Lisa. *With Excellence.* Canada: Ridley Jones Publishing, 2011.

Schwartz, David J. *The Magic of Thinking Big.* Englewood Cliffs, NJ: Prentice-Hall, Inc., 1959.

Seligman, PhD, Martin E.P. *Authentic Happiness.* New York: Simon & Schuster, Inc., 2002.

United HealthCare. (n.d.). Retrieved from http://www.unitedhealth-group.com/news/rel2010/UHC-VolunteerMatch-Survey-Fact-Sheet.pdf

About the Author

After a sales career spanning more than twenty years, Lisa Ryan transformed herself into the Chief Appreciation Strategist and Founder of Grategy®. She is a dynamic inspirational communicator who presents keynotes, workshops and seminars on harnessing the power of gratitude in business and in life.

Lisa has been speaking professionally since 1997. She is featured in the movie "The Keeper of the Keys" with other internationally known self-development experts including: Jack Canfield of *Chicken Soup for the Soul*, Marci Shimoff of *The Secret*, and John Gray of *Men are from Mars; Women are from Venus*.

In 2012, Lisa was featured in the self-development film, "The Gratitude Experiment." She appeared alongside Bob Proctor, Dr. John DeMartini, Mary Morrissey and others from the book and hit movie "The Secret."

She is a professional member of the National Speakers Association, and serves on the Ohio Chapter Board as Protrack Manager. She is also a member of Toastmasters International and holds both a Bachelor's Degree and an MBA in marketing.

In addition to Grategy®, she is the Co-Founder of the Positive Thinkers Network. A Cleveland native, she has been blissfully married to Scott Ryan since 1996.

For further information about Lisa and Grategy®, please visit: www.grategy.com. Lisa can also be contacted at lisa@grategy.com

Quick Order Form:

Order The Upside of Down Times for your next conference, retreat, training or any event where inspiration is needed.

Quantity pricing for direct purchase of the book.
All discounts are savings from the retail price of $19.95.

25 – 100	$17.00 each
101 – 250	$16.00 each
251 - 499	$15.00 each
500 – 999	12.00 each
1000+	10.00 each

Prices do not include freight and handling.
Call for a complete pricing proposal or an estimate to your location.

Call or Email: (216) 225-8027; lisa@grategy.com

Please send me _____ books.
Name:_____
Address:_____
City:_____State:_____
Zip Code:_____
Telephone:_____
Email address:_____

Fax order to (440) 237-2754
Mail Order to: Lisa Ryan
3222 Perl Ct., North Royalton, OH 44133
Visit our website for all the latest news:
www.grategy.com

Hire Lisa Ryan for your next event:

Keynote presentations

Your company, trade association, networking organization, or other group will receive a jolt of energy by hosting Lisa as a keynote speaker. These presentations range from 30 to 90 minutes and can be customized to fit your audience's needs.

Performance Workshops & Seminars

These hands-on interactive sessions are customized to the unique requirements of the host group, and typically run half a day. They offer an immersion experience in the transformative power of gratitude to change lives and organizations. Programs include:

- *"Harnessing the Power of Gratitude"*
  Shows the benefits of gratitude in the areas of Self, Health, Relationships with Others and Wealth

- *"Take Your Thanks to the Bank"*
  Concentrates on the business of gratitude from both customer and employee retention to achieving increased bottom line results

- **"Opting for Optimism"**
  Explores the mental and physical benefits of gratitude

- **"I Appreciate You"**
  Reveals relationship deepening techniques through two "magic words"

For pricing and availability, please call (216) 225-8027 or email lisa@grategy.com. Visit our website at www.grategy.com

CPSIA information can be obtained at www.ICGtesting.com
Printed in the USA
LVOW06s1615060514

384630LV00002B/617/P